Mountains and Rivers Sutra
Teachings by Norman Fischer

A Weekly Practice Guide

Transcribed and Edited by Kuya

MOUNTAINS AND RIVERS SUTRA
Teachings by Norman Fischer
A Weekly Practice Guide
Transcribed and edited by Nora Minogue

Mountains and Rivers Sutra Text © San Francisco Zen Center, 2020
Teachings Text © Upaya Zen Center, 2020
Practice Text © Nora Minogue, 2020
All rights reserved

Design: John Negru
Cover illustration: Shek-wing Tam
Author photo courtesy of Norman Fischer
Editor photo courtesy of Nora Minogue

Published by
The Sumeru Press Inc.
Ottawa, ON
Canada

LIBRARY AND ARCHIVES CANADA CATALOGUING IN PUBLICATION

Title: Mountains and rivers sutra : teachings by Norman Fischer : a weekly practice guide /
   transcribed and edited by Nora Minogue.
Names: Fischer, Norman, 1946- author. | Minogue, Nora, 1946- editor.
Identifiers: Canadiana 20200183265 | ISBN 9781896559582 (softcover)
Subjects: LCSH: Fischer, Norman, 1946- —Teachings. | LCSH: Dōgen, 1200-1253. | LCSH: Enlightenment
   (Zen Buddhism) | LCSH: Spiritual life—Zen Buddhism.
Classification: LCC BQ9288 .F57 2020 | DDC 294.3/927—dc23

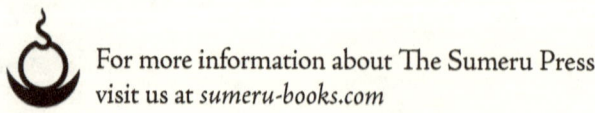

For more information about The Sumeru Press
visit us at *sumeru-books.com*

....

With deep respect and gratitude
to the San Francisco Zen Centre,
for permission to copy
the translation of Dogen's essay,
to the Upaya Zen Centre
who gave permission to use
their recordings of
Norman's words,
to the women
who joined this practice
with their reflections,
and to Norman Fischer
for these magnificent teachings.

....

All royalties from by this book
will be divided between
each of those Zen Centres.

....

> Wherever there is a world of sentient beings,
> there is a world of buddha ancestors.
> Thoroughly examine the meaning of this.
> *Dogen*

Contents

9   Foreword

11   Putting the Book into Practice

13   Mountains and Rivers Sutra

23   The Essays, Practice Suggestions and Responses

129   Afterword

Foreword

IN 2015 AND 2016, I transcribed talks about Dogen's *Mountains and Rivers Sutra* that Norman Fischer gave at the Upaya Zen Centre in 2012. I divided his talks into 52 short essays, added a practice suggestion to each essay and published them in my bimonthly column, "A Zen's Eye View" in our local newspaper. The *Creston Valley Advance* is the weekly rag of Creston, British Columbia, the small rural town where I am resident priest at a backyard lay practice temple called Sakuraji. Local response to the *Mountains and Rivers Sutra* series was overwhelmingly positive.

Creston is a small farming community located in the Kootenay region of southern British Columbia, about a 10-minute drive from the Idaho border. The town's population borders on 5,000. Before we founded Sakuraji in Creston, there was little direct contact with Asian religions such as Soto Zen Buddhism. The primary religious orientation in Creston roots into traditional Christian teachings.

I started the column in 2008, and in the beginning, I presented Zen teachings without reference to Buddhism or to Zen. It was basically a self-help column based on Zen principles. But by 2015, the practice at Sakuraji had attracted a core group of Zen students, and it became a popular place to participate in traditional Zen practice, yoga glasses, qigong classes, writing practice and courses on mindfulness.

After a short break from writing the column, I decided to produce a column that contained more traditional Zen teachings. At the time, I was deep into a study of Dogen's, *Mountains and Rivers Sutra*. In my research about this text, I discovered Norman Fischer's online dharma talks on the Upaya Zen Centre website. There were eleven talks from a retreat called, "Awesome Presence: Dogen's *Mountains and Rivers Sutra*." I transcribed all eleven talks and broke sections of them into column length essays. After each essay, I added a practice suggestion that readers, if interested, could explore over the two weeks between columns.

By early 2016, the column was extremely popular and people were trying out the Suggested Practices. In our local grocery store, at our Saturday Farmer's Market, and at the community swimming pool, people of all walks of life, religious backgrounds and ages would approach me to discuss a practice that they had tried. Some who had followed the suggestion to walk in the mountains paying close attention to their own walking proclaimed that "Mountains really do walk." Others began a meditation practice and began to show up at Sakuraji for Zen practice instruction and support.

It occurred to me that it would be good if these columns could have wider distribution. It was apparent that there was great benefit to the readers to have time between columns to try out and reflect on the practice suggestions. Consequently, this book is divided into 52 short readings, each followed by a practice suggestion written by myself.

One reading represents one week of practice. Consequently, this is not a book to sit down and read from beginning to end, although it's good to do that. This is the book to keep on a bedside table or close to the toilet so it can be read daily. Rereading each essay deepens and extends its impact.

The teachings in this book are not my own; they are Norman Fischer's. I selected the readings based on my own limited understanding at the time. I do not claim to have transmitted to you the full depth of Dogen's or Norman's mind. I'm sure I missed a lot. I take full responsibility if I have inadvertently misrepresented Norman's view.

When I asked Norman about using his words, he said that they were not his words, but the words of his teachers, and claimed no ownership over them. Dogen's words are in the indented passages. The practice suggestions are mine.

Putting the Book into Practice

How many times have I started a project that I hoped would last for a year but fell away after one or two, or even six months? This workbook invites the reader into a committed year-long Zen-based practice. It is so much easier to keep a long-term commitment if there are others training to keep the same commitment, so it will help to get a group together, face-to-face or online, if you want to try out this practice.

To test out the text, I invited several women to join a year-long project that involved reading each essay and responding to it in an email group. I've had an email zen practice on-the-go for close to 20 years. It started in the year 2000, when I was living in Qikituarjaq, Nunavut and working as an adult educator for Nunavut Artic College. I don't remember how the first email Zen practice group started, but while I was in Qikituarjaq I facilitated about seven women in an internet-adapted version of a Zen temple, which I named, Amazenji. Group members lived in locations as far apart as the Northeast coast of the Davis Strait, Kenya and Australia. When we did asynchronous online retreats, checking in by email, I sensed a wave of practice flowing from 5:30 am in Kenya to 5:30 am in Australia.

Four of the five women whom I invited to do the *Mountains and Rivers Practice Book* completed all the readings and responded to most of the practice suggestions for 52 weeks. I sent out each week's reading on a Tuesday, we read it, and wrote a response to it – no rules but limits to length. We didn't discuss each other's writings, but instead picked one to three phrases that drew our attention from each other's responses, – no editing – and fed them back to the group as collage poems.

For example, using the second paragraph above:

> how it started
> nunavut
> kenya and australia

Following some of the short essays and practice sessions below, you will find examples of responses that two of us shared. Two women chose not to have their words included. The responses are in a slightly smaller font than the main text.

What follows is, in itself, a Zen practice. Sustaining practice is always easier when done with others, as we have done here. May you feel encouraged to form your own email group or face-to-face group to share your experience with others.

Mountains and Rivers Sutra

Mountains and Rivers Sutra

MOUNTAINS AND WATERS right now actualize the ancient buddha expression. Each abiding in its condition, unfolds its full potential. Because mountains and waters have been active since before the Empty Eon, they are alive at this moment. Because they have been the self since before form arose, they are emancipation actualized.

Because mountains are high and broad, their way of riding the clouds always extends from the mountains; their wondrous power of soaring in the wind comes freely from the mountains.

· · · · · · · · ·

Priest Daokai of Mount Furong said to the assembly, "The green mountains are always walking; a stone woman gives birth at night."

Mountains do not lack the characteristics of mountains. Therefore, they always abide in ease and always walk. Examine in detail the characteristics of the mountains' walking.

Mountains' walking is just like human walking. Accordingly, do not doubt mountains' walking even through it does not look the same as human walking. The buddha ancestor's words point to walking. This is fundamental understanding. Penetrate these words.

Because green mountains walk, they are permanent. Although they walk more swiftly than the wind, someone in the mountains does not notice or understand it. "In the mountains" means the blossoming of the entire world. People outside the mountains do not notice or understand the mountains' walking. Those without eyes to see mountains cannot notice, understand, see, or hear this reality.

If you doubt mountains' walking, you do not know your own walking; it is not that you do not walk, but that you do not know or understand your own walking. Since you do know your own walking you should fully know the green mountains' walking.

Green mountains are neither sentient nor insentient. You are neither sentient nor insentient. At this moment, you cannot doubt the green mountains' walking.

· · · · · · · · ·

You may not notice that you study the green mountains, using numerous worlds of phenomena as your standards. Clearly examine the green mountains' walking and your own walking. Examine walking backward and backward walking, and investigate the fact that walking forward and backward has never stopped since the very moment before form arose, since the time of the King of the Empty Eon.

If walking had stopped, buddha ancestors would not have appeared. If walking ends, the buddha dharma cannot reach the present. Walking forward does not cease; walking backward does not cease. Walking forward does not obstruct walking backward. Walking backward does not obstruct walking forward. This is called the mountains' flow and the flowing mountains.

· · · · · · · ·

Green mountains thoroughly practice walking and eastern mountains thoroughly practice travelling on water. Accordingly, these activities are a mountain's practice. Keeping its own form, without changing body and mind, a mountain always practices in every place.

Don't slander by saying that a green mountain cannot walk and an eastern mountain cannot travel on water. When your understanding is shallow, you doubt the phrase *Green mountains are always walking*. When your learning is immature, you are shocked by the words *flowing mountains*. Without even understanding the words *flowing water*, you drown in small views and narrow understanding.

Yet the characteristics of mountains manifest their form and life force. There is walking, there is flowing, and there is a moment when a mountain gives birth to a mountain child. Because mountains are buddha ancestors, buddha ancestors appear in this way.

Even if you have an eye to see mountains as grass, trees, earth, rocks or walls, do not be confused or swayed by it; this is not complete realization. Even if there is a moment when you view mountains as the seven treasures' splendor, this is not returning to the source. Even if you understand mountains as the realm where all buddhas practice, this understanding is not something to be attached to. Even if you have the highest understanding of mountains as all buddhas' wondrous characteristics, the truth is not only this. These are conditioned views. This is not the understanding of buddha ancestors, but merely looking through a bamboo pipe at a corner of the sky.

Turning the circumstances and turning mind is rejected by the great sage. Speaking of mind and speaking of essence is not agreeable to buddha ancestors. Seeing into mind and seeing into essence is the activity of people outside the way. Confined words and phrases to do not lead to liberation. There is something free from all of these views. That is: *Green mountains are always walking and Eastern mountains travel on water*. Study this in detail.

· · · · · · · ·

A stone woman gives birth to a child at night means that the moment when a barren woman gives birth to a child is called night.

There are male stones, female stones, nonmale, nonfemale stones. Placed in the sky and in the earth, they are called heavenly stones and earthly stones. These are explained in the ordinary world, but not many people know about it.

Understand the meaning of *gives birth to a child*. At the moment of giving birth to a child, is the mother separate from the child? Study not only that you become a mother when your child is born, but also that you become a child. This is to actualize giving birth in practice realization. Study and investigate this thoroughly.

· · · · · · · ·

Yunmen, Great Master Kuangzhen, said, "Eastern mountains travel on water." The meaning of these words brought forth that all mountains are eastern mountains, and all eastern mountains travel on water. Because of this, Nine Mountains, Mount Sumeru, and other mountains appear and have practice realization. These are called *eastern mountains*. However, could Yunmen penetrate the skin, flesh, bones, and marrow of the eastern mountains and their vital practice-realization?

·········

Now, in Great Song China there are careless fellows who form groups; they cannot be set straight by the few true masters. They say that the statement "Eastern mountains travel on water," or Nanquan's story of a sickle, is illogical; what they mean is that any words having to do with logical thought are not buddha ancestors' Zen words, and that only illogical stories are buddha ancestors' expressions. In this way, they consider Huangbo's striking with a staff and Linji's shout as beyond logic and unconcerned with thought; they regard these as words of great enlightenment that precede the arising of form.

They say, "Ancient masters used expedient phrases, which are beyond understanding, to slash entangled vines." Those who say this have never seen a true master, and they have no eye of understanding. They are immature, foolish fellows not even worth discussing. In China, these two or three hundred years, there have been many groups of demons and six types of heretical thinkers. What a pity! The great road of buddha ancestors is crumbling. People who hold this view are not even as good as shravakas of the Lesser Vehicles and are more foolish than those outside the way. They are neither laypeople nor monks, neither humans not heavenly beings. They are more stupid than animals that learn the buddha way.

The illogical stories mentioned by those bald-headed fellows are only illogical for them, not for buddha ancestors. Even though they do not understand, they should not neglect studying the buddha ancestors' path of understanding. Even if it is beyond understanding in the end, their present understanding is off the mark.

I have personally seen and heard many people like this in Song China. How sad that they do not know about the phrases of logical thought or penetrating logical thought in phrases! When I laughed at them in China, they had no response and remained silent. Their idea about illogical words is only a distorted view. Even if there is no teacher to show them the original truth, their belief in spontaneous enlightenment is a view of those outside the way.

·········

Know that *eastern mountains travel on water* is the bones and marrow of the buddha ancestors. All waters appear at the foot of the eastern mountains. Accordingly, all mountains ride on clouds and walk in the sky. All mountains are the tops of the heads of all waters. Walking beyond and walking within are both done on water. All mountains walk with their toes on waters and make them splash. Thus, in walking there are seven vertical paths and eight horizontal paths. This is practice realization.

·········

Water is neither strong nor weak, neither wet nor dry, neither moving nor still, neither cold nor hot, neither existent nor nonexistent, neither deluded nor enlightened. When water solidifies, it is harder than a diamond. Who can crack it? When water melts, it is softer than milk. Who can destroy it? Do not doubt that these are the characteristics water manifests. Reflect on the moment when you see water of the ten directions as water of the ten directions.

This is not merely studying the moment when human and heavenly beings see water; this is studying the moment when water sees water. Because water practices and realizes water, water expresses water. Actualize the path where self encounters self. Go forward and backward, leaping beyond the vital path where other fathoms other.

· · · · · · · · ·

Not all beings see mountains and waters in the same way. Some beings see water as a jeweled ornament, but they do not regard jeweled ornaments as water. What in the human realm corresponds to their water? We only see their jeweled ornaments as water.

Some beings see water as wondrous blossoms, but they do not use blossoms as water. Hungry ghosts see water as raging fire or pus and blood. Dragons and fish see water as a palace or a pavilion. Some beings see water as the seven treasures or a wish-granting jewel. Some being see water as a forest or a wall. Some see it is the dharma nature of pure liberation, the true human body, or the form of the body and the essence of mind. Human beings see water as water. Water is seen as dead or alive depending on [the seer's] causes and conditions.

Thus, the views of all beings are not the same. Question this matter now. Are there many ways to see one thing, or is it a mistake to see many forms as one thing? Pursue this beyond the limit of pursuit. Accordingly, endeavors in practice-realization of the way are not limited to one or two kinds. The thoroughly actualized realm has one thousand kinds and ten thousand ways.

When we think about the meaning of this, it seems that there is water for various beings but there is no original water — there is no water common to all types of beings. But water for these various kinds of beings does not depend on mind or body, does not arise from actions, does not depend on self or other. Water's freedom depends only on water.

In this way, water is not just earth, water, fire, wind, space of consciousness. Water is not blue, yellow, red white, or black. Water is not form, sound, smell, taste, touch, or mind. But water as earth, water, fire, wind, and space actualizes itself.

This being so, it is difficult to say who has created this land and palace right now or how such things have been created. To say that the world is resting on the wheel of space or on the wheel of wind is not the truth of the self or the truth of others. Such a statement is based only on a small view of assumptions. People speak this way because they think that it is impossible for things to exist without having place to rest.

· · · · · · · · ·

The Buddha said, "All things are ultimately unbound. There is nowhere that they permanently abide."

Know that even though all things are unbound and not tied to anything, they abide in their own condition. However, when most human beings see water, they only see that it flows unceasingly. This is a limited human view; there are actually many kinds of flowing. Water flows on the earth, in the sky, upward, downward. It flows around a single curve or into many bottomless abysses. When it rises, it becomes clouds. When it descends, it forms abysses.

·········

Wenzi said, "The path of water is such that when it rises to the sky, it becomes raindrops; when it falls to the ground, it becomes rivers."

Even a secular person can speak this way. You who call yourselves descendants of buddha ancestors should feel ashamed of being more ignorant than an ordinary person. The path of water is not noticed by water but is actualized by water.

When it rises to the sky, it becomes raindrops means that water rises to the heavens and skies and forms raindrops. Raindrops vary according to different worlds. To say that there are places water does not reach is the teaching of the shravakas in the Lesser Vehicles or the mistaken teaching of people outside the way. Water exists inside fire and inside mind, thought, and discernment. Water also reaches inside realization of buddha nature.

When it falls to the ground, it becomes rivers means that when water reaches the ground it turns into rivers. The essence of the rivers becomes a wise person.

Ordinary fools and mediocre people nowadays think that water is always in rivers or oceans, but this is not so. There are rivers and oceans within water. Thus, even where there is not a river or an ocean, there is water. It is just that when water falls down to the ground, it manifests the characteristics of rivers and oceans.

Also, do not think that where water forms rivers or oceans there is no world and there is no buddha land. Even in a drop of water innumerable buddha lands appear. Accordingly, it is not that there is only water in the buddha land or a buddha land in water.

Where water abides is not concerned with the past, future, present, or the worlds of phenomena. Yet, water is the fundamental point actualized. Where buddha ancestors reach, water never fails to reach. Where water reaches, buddha ancestors never fail to be present. Thus, buddha ancestors always take up water and make it their body and mind, make it their thought.

In this way, the words *Water does not rise* are not found in scriptures inside or outside [of buddha dharma]. The path of water runs upward, downward and in all directions.

However, one buddha sutra does say, *Fire and air go upward, earth and water go downward.* This *upward* and *downward* require examination. Examine this from the point of view of the buddha way. Although you use the word *downward* to describe the direction earth and water go, earth and water do not actually go downward. In the same way, the direction fire and air go is called *upward*.

The world of phenomena is not limited by up, down, or the cardinal directions. They are tentatively designated according to the directions in which four great elements, five great elements, or six great elements go. The Heaven of No Thought should not be regarded as *upward* nor should Avichi Hell be regarded as *downward*. The Avichi Hell is the entire world of phenomena; the Heaven of No Thought is the entire world of phenomena.

· · · · · · · · ·

Now, when dragons and fish see water as a palace, it may be like human beings seeing a palace. They may not think it flows. If an outsider tells them, "What you see as a palace is running water," the dragons and fish may be astonished, just as we are when we hear the words *Mountains flow*. Nevertheless, there may be some dragons and fish who understand that the railings and pillars of palaces and pavilions are flowing water.

Quietly reflect and ponder the meaning of this. If you do not learn to penetrate your superficial views, you will not be free from the body and mind of an ordinary person. Then you will not thoroughly experience the land of buddha ancestors, or even the land or the palace of ordinary people.

At this time, human beings deeply know that what is in the ocean and the river is water, but do not know what dragons and fish see and use as water. Do not foolishly suppose that what we see as water is used as water by all other beings. You who study with buddhas should not be limited to human views when you see water. Go further and study water in the buddha way. Study how you view the water used by buddha ancestors. Study whether there is water or no water in the house of buddha ancestors.

· · · · · · · · ·

Mountains have been the abodes of great sages from the limitless past to the limitless present. Wise people and sages all have mountains as their inner chamber, as their body and mind. Because of wise people and sages, mountains are actualized.

You may think that in mountains many wise people and great sages are assembled. But after entering the mountain not a single person meets another. There is just the vital activity of the mountains. There is no trace of anyone having entered the mountains.

When you see mountains from the ordinary world, and when you meet mountains while in mountains, the mountains' head and eye are viewed quite differently. Your idea or view of mountains not flowing is not the same as the view of dragons and fish. Human and heavenly beings have attained a position concerning their own worlds that other being may doubt or may not have the capacity to doubt.

Do not remain bewildered and skeptical when you hear the words *Mountains flow*; but study these words with buddha ancestors. When you take up one view, you see mountains flowing, and when you take up another view, mountains are not flowing. One time mountains are flowing; another time they are not flowing. If you do not fully understand this, you do not understand the true dharma wheel of the Tathagata.

An ancient buddha said, "If you do not wish to incur the cause for Unceasing Hell, do not slander the true dharma wheel of the Tathagata." Carve these words on your skin, flesh, bones and marrow; on your body, mind and environs; on emptiness and on form. They are already carved on trees and rocks, on fields and villages.

....

Although mountains belong to the nation, mountains belong to people who love them. When mountains love their master, such a virtuous sage of wise person enters the mountains. Since mountains belong to the sages and wise people living there, trees and rocks become abundant and birds and animals are inspired. This is so because sages and wise people extend their virtue.

Know for a fact that mountains are fond of wise people and sages. Rulers have visited mountains to pay homage to wise people or to ask for instructions from great sages. These have been excellent precedents in the past and present. At such times these rulers treat the sages as teachers, disregarding the protocol of the usual world. Their imperial power has no authority over the wise people in the mountains. Mountains are apart from the human world. At the time the Yellow Emperor visited Mount Kongdong to pay homage to Guangcheng, he walked on his knees, touched his forehead to the ground and asked for instruction.

When Shakyamuni Buddha left his father's palace and entered the mountains, his father, the king, did not resent the mountains, nor was he suspicious of those who taught the prince in the mountains. The twelve years of Shakyamuni Buddha's practice of the way were mostly spent in the mountains, and his opening of way occurred in the mountains. Thus, even his father, a wheel-turning king, did not wield authority in the mountains.

Know that mountains are not the realm of human beings or the realm of heavenly beings. Do not view mountains from the standard of human thought. If you do not judge mountains' flowing by the human understanding of flowing, you will not doubt mountains' flowing and not flowing.

....

On the other hand, from ancient times wise people and sages have often lived on water. When they live on water, they catch fish, catch human beings and catch the way. These were all ancient ways of being on water, following wind and streams. Furthermore, there is catching the self, catching catching, being caught by catching and being caught by the way.

Priest Decheng abruptly left Mount Yao and lived on the river. There he produced a successor, the wise sage of the Huating River [Jishan Shanhui]. Is this not catching a fish, catching a person, catching water or catching the self? The disciple seeing Decheng is Decheng. Decheng guiding his disciple is meeting a [true] person.

....

It is not only that there is water in the world, but there is a world in water. It is not merely in water. There is a world of sentient beings in clouds. There is a world of sentient beings in the air. There is a world of sentient beings in fire. There is a world of sentient beings on earth. There is a world of sentient beings in the world of phenomena. There is a world of sentient beings in a blade of grass. There is a world of sentient beings in one staff.

Wherever there is a world of sentient beings, there is a world of buddha ancestors. Thoroughly examine the meaning of this.

....

In this way, water is the true dragon's palace. It is not flowing downward. To regard water as only flowing is to slander water with the word *flowing*. This would be the same as insisting that water does not flow.

Water is just the true thusness of water. Water is water's complete characteristics; it is not flowing. When you investigate the flowing and not-flowing of a handful of water, thorough experience of all things is immediately actualized.

....

There are mountains hidden in treasures. There are mountains hidden in swamps. There are mountains hidden in the sky. There are mountains hidden in mountains. There are mountains hidden in hiddenness. This is how we study.

An ancient buddha said, "Mountains are mountains, waters are waters." These words do not mean mountains are mountains; they mean mountains are mountains.

In this way, investigate mountains thoroughly. When you investigate mountains thoroughly, this becomes the endeavor within the mountains.

Such mountains and waters of themselves become wise persons and sages.

Presented to the assembly at Kannondori Kosho Horin Monastery at the hour of the Rat [midnight], the eighteenth day, the tenth month, the first year of the Ninji Era [1240]

The Essays, Practice Suggestions and Responses

Week 1

Traditional Zen Teaching

THE MOUNTAINS AND RIVERS SUTRA is one of 93 essays of Dogen that have been collected in a work called, The *Shobogenzo*. "Shobogenzo" means, "Treasury of the True Dharma Eye." In other words, the essays in the *Shobogenzo* are Dogen's attempt to express the reality of the enlightened mind. They are not easy to read because they are full of references to the Zen teachings of the past, and often obscurely poetic. Dogen was very well-versed in the ancient teachings and referred to them often as he attempted to translate them into a language that his contemporaries would understand. I will try to translate Dogen's medieval essays into a language understandable to we who live in the 21st Century. This undertaking is a humbling experience, but I will do the best I can.

The word "sutra" usually refers to words that the Buddha actually spoke when he was alive in 5th Century BCE. His words were passed on orally for 500 years and then transcribed into written documents by his students around 100 CE. His teachings have been passed on through many generations of Buddhist practitioners. Dogen transmitted these teachings through direct teaching and though his writings.

In his essay, as he often does, Dogen uses words in a way that is different from their usual use, thus expanding their meaning and deepening their context. As mentioned, the word "sutra" for example usually refers to the remembered and recorded words of the historical Buddha, who lived in 5th Century BCE. Dogen is not suggesting that his essay is a "sutra," and therefore the words of a Buddha. Instead, he is making the astonishing statement that the activities and sounds of mountains and rivers are, in themselves, a sutra, because they perfectly express the essence of the teachings of the historical Buddha. In this essay, *Mountains and Rivers Sutra*, Dogen is explaining what it is that mountains and rivers are teaching us.

Suggested Practice:
Traditional Zen Teaching

Take some time to go for a walk, preferably on a mountain trail by a creek. Listen to the sounds that arise in awareness. As you walk, notice when your mind wanders to the past or future and gently coax your attention back to awareness of the sound of the mountains and waters. Don't label or analyze; just listen.

·········

Corn snow is falling as I walk down to the stream; deer tracks lead into the forest (I am not alone). I stop, breathing in the cold air; the flow of water dominates the world. I start to walk; it is very slippery (I must pay attention). I move up, farther on to the bank and stop, listening to the sound of squirrels chattering (like my monkey mind). As I walk up the stream, the flow has narrowed and quickened (I am closer to the source). I am walking into a mist (and realize I sleep-walk through life). My task was to listen and learn, not analyze. As a novice to this work, I keep moving between the forest, water and my mind. I have a lot of work to do as I have not surrendered to the task.

·········

I am nothing more than a drop of fresh water flowing from mountain glacier to lake.

Food and flesh. It's all water. Born as glacial ice, sun melts me off the glacier edge. I fall into a tiny stream bubbling up from between two sharp-edged rocks. I travel in rills and runnels, in rivulets and creeks, until I enter a quiet lake, stir things up, and then settle down into practice, into writing practice, donning my writing practice rakusu with "Sit, Walk, Write." And now, listening to this pen scratch across this blank page, noticing heart/chest filling with excitement to be sharing this practice with you.

Week 2

Enlightenment Is Here/Now

IN *MOUNTAINS AND RIVERS SUTRA*, Dogen expressed a viewpoint that was different from other Buddhist teachings popular in Japan in the 13th Century. Indeed, he takes other teachers to task for teaching that meditation practice will eventually lead to enlightenment.

"Others have it wrong," he said, "They are not seeing the wholeness of reality. They are seeing it only partially." Dogen learned this from his Chinese teacher, Rujing, during the five years that he trained in China. He was not making it up himself.

The main difference between other medieval Zen teachings and Dogen's teaching is that, for Dogen, Zen training is not a developmental training process with the goal of enlightenment. The Zen path does not go from ignorance to knowledge, from unenlightenment to enlightenment. Dogen saw Zen training as a practice that enables us to live life fully, every day, starting today. For Dogen, enlightenment is present in every single moment. It is not a special moment where you suddenly have an "aha" experience that you have been seeking. It is simply whole-hearted participation in every moment, without anything left out. To Dogen, Zen practice is enlightenment and it's happening here and now. It isn't something that happens later.

Dogen insisted that we all have Buddha nature – that is, we are already enlightened; we just don't know it. And because we don't know it, we live in way that is destructive and that cuts us off from true intimacy. We come by this alienation honestly. It's in our education, our culture, our society and our families. It's normal to make the mistake of trying to add something to, or take something away from, what is already here, but it is still a mistake.

In other words, Dogen believed that we are not appreciating what life actually is. Zen practice is nothing more than appreciating life as it is, and then living it fully every moment. The current self-help culture drives us towards future conditions and encourages us to look beyond this moment for something that we don't already possess. Because of this tendency, we are always looking at things, including spiritual experience, with desire and expectation. We are never quite complete.

But Dogen says no. Right now, step inside your life and let go of all conceptual frameworks that alienate you from yourself, and from each other. Just enter life completely in this very moment. Feel the awesome presence of what you can hear, see, smell, taste and touch right now. Become aware of emotions, thoughts, memories and dreams that flood awareness without getting hooked by any of them. Feel how, right now, human experience is truly awesome, and don't look for something to complete what is already complete.

But most often, we don't believe that everything we need is right here, right now. We are always looking for something more than what we have – something that is missing.

This idea summarizes the unique approach to Zen that Dogen clearly expressed in "Mountains and River Sutra." He is not saying that there is no path and no destination; but he is saying that the destination is at every point along the path. We are not marching through time to get to a destination because there is both path and destination in every moment.

Suggested Practice:
Enlightenment Is Here/Now

For the next week, each time you leave your house, stop for five minutes, raise your eyes to the mountains or to a distant horizon and wonder at their perfection. How does the air feel on your skin, in your nostrils? How does raising your eyes up to the hills and taking time to abide in that place affect your state of mind? How is your life awesome in this very moment?

· · · · · · · · ·

"Live life fully." Does that mean realizing a reality deeper than sensory experience, a reality that underlies everything, a reality in which mountains walk and stone woman gives birth to a child at night?

It is cold, I am shoveling snow, a heavy, wet, slippery snow that covers my deck, my garden.

The garden is still hosting life as birds feed off the remains of the elderberries, cat tracks wander through the snow on the path from the back yard. I don't know this cat but the cat knows my yard. Stop and breathe the cold air and return to myself. The snow is turning to rain.

Week 3

Listen to Mountains and Rivers

Long before Buddhism came to China in 200 CE, Taoist sages realized the power, depth and profundity of mountains and rivers. They recognized that the two are interdependent. Mountains create rivers, and the constant movement of glaciers, rivers of ice, creates mountains. In fact, in the Chinese language, "mountains and rivers" is often used as the word for "nature." For ancient Taoists, there is a deep sanity that transcends human thought in the mountains and rivers. For this reason, Taoist monks often left the constant bickering and fighting over access to fame and gain in the cities to follow the path of the clouds. Here they found tender benevolence and a logic that transcends human suffering.

Something deep in us resonates with that. The essence of nature resides in our human hearts, and most of us know that we need contact with nature to be whole. Many people have told Zen teachers that they find spiritual truth through hiking or camping, or by just sitting in nature. This has been the case through many cultures, religions and times. Moses communed with the God of his understanding on a mountain; Rumi, the Sufi poet, praised the wildness of mountains and rivers. In our own time, the back-to-the-land movement of the 1960s took adults out of the cities and into the rural areas to try to live closer to nature. All of these activities reflect the idea that life in nature transcends life in the city.

For Dogen, this transcendence is evoked in the presence of mountains and rivers. Mountains seem to be eternal. The mountains have been here for millions of years. They never seem to move. They are constant. They were here 10,000 years ago when North America was inhabited by the aboriginal nations; they were here when European explorers passed by them as they paddled down North America's rivers in the early 1800s; and they are here, now, each time we turn our gaze towards their peaks. Water, on the other hand is always moving. Many separate rivers have travelled from distant places to meet in fertile valleys. They rise from the mountain springs and glaciers in the high alpine and flow downwards until meeting a major river. From this confluence, they bend and wind through many miles and finally enter an ocean. In Buddhist teachings mountains often represent form, and water represents emptiness. Water has no permanent form. It can be a river, a lake, a cloud, a dewdrop or an ocean. Mountains, on the other hand appear to hold the same form over long stretches of time.

When Dogen chose the title for the essay *Mountains and Rivers Sutra*, he was probably thinking of a famous poem by the Song dynasty poet, Sudong Bo, a 12th Century Buddhist monk who lived in a mountain hermitage high in the mountains of China. One night, in an experience of true transcendence, Sudong Bo stayed up from dusk until dawn meditating. In the morning, he wrote:

> The stream with its sounds is his long broad tongue
> The looming mountain his wide-awake body

Throughout the night song after song
How can I speak at dawn?

Sudong Bo is saying that the sound of the stream is the essence of Buddha's teaching, for which language is a crude container. For Sudong Bo, the body of Buddha is not the body of the historical Buddha who lived in 6th Century BCE. For Sudong Bo, and for Dogen, mountains and rivers are the body and tongue of Buddha. The essay, *Mountains and Rivers Sutra*, is Dogen's attempt to translate the profound teachings of the mountains and rivers into words.

Suggested Practice:
Listen to Mountains and Rivers

If you can, take some time this week to visit the confluence place of two nearby rivers. Listen to the sounds all around you. Be aware of sounds that come from the water and sounds that come from the mountains. What do the mountains and rivers tell you? What teachings are they expressing? Consider how impossible it is to put these teachings into words.

·········

> I live on the shore of Lake Pend Oreille, the remains of an old glacier path, now filled by the confluence of two rivers – The Clark Fork River that flows in from Montana, and the Pack River that flows in from the Selkirks.
> I am reminded of a Sufi story I once heard.

They watch the river disappear in the sand and say there it goes
The clouds watch and say here it comes
Today it is snowing
Tonight it will freeze
Tomorrow it rains
Water flowing down from the sky
Down my street
Into the stream, the lake and on to the ocean
I am water
Flowing back to the source
Connecting to all life.

·········

During the last heavy snowstorm, I created a huge mountain-shaped snowbank in the temple garden. Every time I pass by it, I notice it has shrunk, and I remember that the glaciers all over the earth are melting. "Water has no permanent form. It can be a lake, a cloud, a dewdrop or an ocean." Inside each dewdrop is an iceberg; in each iceberg, a dewdrop.

Week 4

Mountains Are Mountains

Recall how Sudong Bo, a Song Dynasty poet, after a long night of meditation, experienced the mountains as transcending the ordinary mountains that he had been looking at since childhood. The long night of meditation awakened Sudong Bo from the fixed view of mountains in the past. It wasn't that the mountains looked or sounded different; and yet everything about them, after his night of meditation, was completely different. You may have a feeling for what this is like. It's as if the physical world – sounds, forms and feelings evoke a presence that is beyond the two-dimensional presence we give our ordinary daily lives. At these times, we feel like we have been here before and yet there is something here, that was always here, but we never noticed. It's like we had been dreaming up to this moment, and now, we are finally and fully awake.

In *Mountains and Rivers Sutra,* Dogen is probably thinking about another ancient Chinese saying.

> When I first began to practice, mountains were mountains; rivers were rivers. As I trained, mountains were not mountains; rivers were not rivers. Now that I am established in the way, mountains are once more mountains, and rivers are once again rivers.

These words represent three different ways we feel about our lives. In the first instance, we see mountains and rivers, and other people, only through the lens of our previous conditioning, our projection, our separation and alienation. Everybody is like this. We see things in an oppositional relationship where everything is flat and two dimensional. Life seems hard. Other people are either for us or against us. Time and money are scarce. We have to struggle to get by.

That's the first "Mountains are mountains and rivers are rivers" in which our whole life is limited by our fixed opinions. But at some point, we wake up to the realization that there must be another way of living this life. Zen practices point us toward this other way.

Through practice we realize that everything is impermanent. This doesn't just mean that over time things change; it means that things are changing in every micro-moment. We can't hold on to anything, not even ourselves. The person we imagined ourselves to be yesterday is different today. The person we are when we are forty is different from the person we were when we were fifteen. We can't grasp a thought, or make our breath stay still for longer than a few minutes. They say that every cell in the body changes every seven years. On one hand this can be terrifying. If there is nothing to grasp; everything will be lost.

On other hand, impermanence means that suffering will pass. When we realize this impermanence; mountains are not mountains and rivers are not rivers. They are just passing moments in time, and impermanence is no longer an intellectual concept; it's just the way things are.

At this point, we settle into life as it is. Practice as something special, disappears. There is only life. There are only mountains being mountains, and rivers being rivers in their pristine beauty. At this point, we can fully accept the condition of our lives and realize that the particulars, family, job, and possessions are only a vehicle for how we live out our deepest spiritual values.

Suggested Practice:
Mountains Are Mountains

For the next week, take some time to consider how each of your daily activities – sitting, walking, talking, working, eating, resting – can be an expression of your deepest spiritual values. Bring this to mind from time to time as you move through your day.

・・・・・・・・

In waking
I realize the gift
Today is my 26,709th day on earth
Unfolding myself into the morning
Expecting nothing
Breathing in life
Exhaling a smile
I rejoice in being alive

・・・・・・・・

Sudong, sitting in his mountain cave,
knows that whatever arises in his mind,
is the broad tongue of the buddha
he sees the teachings of tenderness
emanating from a deep, deep sanity
in a long night of silent sitting
amidst swirling, whirling sensations
floating on a saffron ride over green waters
beyond the lightening-edged shadows
to the other side of moving purple mountains.

Week 5

The Earth Breathes Us

When the Chinese encountered the word "dhyana", the Pali word for meditation, they translated it into something that *sounded* like "dhyana" in Chinese. They chose the word "chan" which became "zen" in Japan. But "chan" or "zen" doesn't mean meditation; it only sounds like the Pali word that means meditation. The literal meaning of "chan" is to "bow before mountains and rivers." So, when we sit in Zen meditation, that is what we are doing, bowing before mountains and rivers. The Chinese never looked at meditation as something that is good for our physical and mental health. For them, meditation was simply an expression of spiritual truth. To sit in meditation was to return to the oneness of our original nature.

Sitting meditation is a very physical activity. It is not just a practice of the mind. Experienced meditators develop a deep awareness of subtle changes in their bodies. When we sit, we are like mountains and rivers. We sit strong and tall, like a mountain, and our shape when we are sitting, resembles the shape of a mountain. Our bodies are made mostly of water, and the rivers of our circulatory systems are constantly flowing. Mountain winds move through our lungs, expanding and contracting our chest and abdomen.

We don't usually pay much attention to our bodies unless we are sick. We just assume that our bodies will carry out the activities that support our survival. But the truth is, our bodies have a deep and profound relationship to the earth. We are, like the earth, made up of water, wind, fire and minerals. In fact, we are just another temporary manifestation of the earth.

If we could speed up time, we could see all beings rising up on the earth, leaving the earth and then, returning to the earth. Everything does this. Plants, animals, insects, rocks, even mountains and rivers eventually return to the earth. It's as if the earth is breathing everything out and then back in again. It's not just our thoughts that come and go – it's everything.

When we sit in zazen, we begin to realize that this coming into and moving out of being is actually what is going on all the time. That's what this life is about. This eternal process of taking on and losing shape and form is always going on. When we remember that this body is just a miniscule part of a huge ongoing transformation, we realize how small our lifetime is compared to the enormity of this eternal process. We begin to realize how miraculous it is that we are so well taken care of. We have everything we need and our vital functions happen without our intention. If we had to remember to breathe or remind our hearts to beat, we would all be dead. But this enormous process takes care of it all. We just appeared, and from then on everything has been taking care of us. When we sit in meditation, we are bowing before the kindness of mountains and rivers.

Suggested Practice:
The Earth Breathes Us

At your next meal take the time to notice, really notice, the food in front of you. The food that sustains your life is the product of a process that has been going on from time immemorial. Sun, rain, earth and air have all contributed to your meal. Others have planted it, cultivated it and harvested so you could live. Bow to the kindness of all beings.

• • • • • • • • •

Bowing to the sun, rain, soil and the hands that feed me lunch
Swirling shreds of purple cabbage
Creamy yellow green avocado
Crunchy orange carrots
Robust spinach
Spicy, green arugula
Tart, slippery, garlicky artichokes
Greek olives
White feta
Italian sun olive oil
California zesty lemon
Bowing, bowing, bowing
I smile

Week 6

Everything Is Teaching Us

Mountains and waters right now actualize the ancient Buddha expression. Each, abiding in its condition, unfolds its full potential. Because mountains and waters have been active since before the Empty Eon, they are alive at this moment. Because they have been the self since before form arose, they are emancipation actualized.

DOGEN, AS HE USUALLY DOES in his essays, begins with what he most wants to say. Everything he says after that is further explanation. Here he is saying that mountains and waters, as well as everything that is deep in our hearts, every physical thing, every object that appears – including computers, freeways and cell phones – is a unique expression of the most profound of Buddhist understanding and teachings. Everything is Buddha. Everything expresses the fundamental truth of existence. We think of mountains and waters as a part of something bigger than ordinary reality, but we think of cell phones and computers as objects that are not spiritually significant. But Dogen says that everything that appears expresses the purest and highest truth.

What a great idea! It's stunning to imagine. This is why, in Zen monasteries, you will see monks bowing to objects that they have accidentally bumped. Recent research affirms that trees have a communal consciousness; we have long known that animals have the same. Some would say that even rocks have consciousness. It makes no sense to argue against these ideas.

But it's hard to actually realize this truth. It's easy to say you believe it, but if you observe your thoughts and experiences during a day you will see that you do not actually think it is true. You do not, for example, think that sitting down to lunch is immersing yourself in the truth of existence.

A preference comes up, "I don't like this brown rice; I wanted something else for lunch." But if you realized that brown rice is the absolute manifestation of Buddha's truth, you could never have such a thought. If you realize that all the things you do and all the things you are express the Buddha's spiritual truth, it becomes obvious that at home and at work, you can live a life of deep and constant reverence for the awesome nature of our existence.

Of course, we all have our preferences – it's just natural. But if you were living in the world that Dogen describes, you would have a deep realization of how miraculous it is that we are even here at all. Preferences lose their pull. Every moment contains spiritual truth, but it is difficult to realize that when we sit down and find brown rice on our plate, when we really wanted spaghetti and meatballs. So many of us are dissatisfied because we don't like the rice, or because we want a different car, or a faster computer. We reject what is happening in our life right now. We have forgotten what Dogen is telling us – that mountains and rivers, that is, everything in our lives, is a full expression of deep spiritual teachings.

Suggested Practice:
Everything Is Teaching Us

Imagine that you are completely content with life as it is at this moment. Stop in the middle of some activity and pay attention to your breath, the most constant reality in your life. Take the time to realize the miracle that, once again after breathing out, you have breathed in.

·········

It is morning, it is snowing, I am in the home of a friend. I rise and go to sit by the fire, watching the early morning light move across the snowy deck, feeling the warmth of the fire, smelling the coffee brewing. I am not alone in the house but am alone by the fire, and I sit in gratitude for the warmth, the friendship, the emerging light. I pick up a book of poetry. In this moment, I am totally present, breathing into the dawning light, the warmth; I breathe in gratitude. The phone beeps, my friend comes from her room and reads the text in silence. She brings me coffee, tells me a friend has just passed. We sit in silence watching the fire, breathing in the moment of life.

·········

Contentment sounds like it could be easy, but it is something that I have not truly known until the last year or so. I was always trying to improve myself in some way. Stronger, thinner, more flexible, more graceful, more learned, more charismatic, more authentic, more helpful, more travelled, were ideals that drove me into endless attempts to become more enlightened, more respected, more recognized, more interesting. It was so exhausting.

My partner and I are heading up to a ski mountain with our cross-country skis. We chatted as we packed. In our imagination, we were soaring across mountain meadows, up and down the trail knolls, flying in the wind. Then we just looked at each other and laughed. I am injured in my right foot, have chronic pain in my left hip and lower back pain; my partner is scared of skiing and does not like snow and cold. At the same moment we said, "I'm taking lots of books." I am content with clicking into the skis, swooshing out for a short run and then bundling up in front of the fireplace with a book and a coffee.

Week 7

This Moment Is Exactly Right

MAYBE ONCE OR TWICE in a lifetime we have that wonderful feeling that this place, this person, this moment is exactly right. Everything is just as it should be – full and complete. It's a wonderful feeling, but rare. Usually we struggle for completion and self-improvement. We try to become whole but never quite get there. But, right now, imagine that this moment is exactly complete as it is. Nothing needs to be added; nothing needs to be removed.

When we think of impermanence, we think it means that wonderful experiences disappear before we can grasp them. The spring plum blossoms will soon fall to the ground and decompose. Impermanence seems incomplete to us because we have this habit of grasping at things we can't hold on to. Often it seems like we are losing everything. But true impermanence is actually the opposite of that. With true impermanence, each thing that appears carries the entire profound truth at its moment of appearance. This means that in every moment we can be fully satisfied, fully complete. Isn't that great?

We could call this enlightenment, but that sounds so unattainable. It makes enlightenment into just another object to be grasped after. That's why I hesitate to use the word. Enlightenment is not something you have to make into a goal. Enlightenment is just how things are. It is found in relationships that appear in every moment. We don't have to *get* enlightened. We *are* enlightenment itself, because enlightenment is everything that appears and then disappears.

But we don't often feel like that, so we turn enlightenment into a problem that we have to solve. Our tendency to do that, itself, is a problem, because it makes us dissatisfied with our life, as our life is, right now. It wouldn't be so bad if the only result was that we feel unhappy; but we do a lot of stupid things when we are unhappy, and because we don't know who we are, we destroy relationships, or we spend a lot of time trying to get material things we imagine will bring contentment. In doing that to excess, we end up destroying the earth.

This is the situation Zen students are trying to resolve when they meditate. Each time we sit in meditation we come closer to realizing what is true and real. We can't be destructive to relationships or to the planet when sitting in silence. Living a life in which meditation is the primary touchstone is a beautiful possibility. And we can all do that right here in our homes and communities. We don't have to live in a Zen monastery where everything is designed to constantly point to truth in every moment. If we practice meditation regularly, we begin to realize spiritual truth as the basis of our lives.

It's a mistake to think that meditation is something we do to calm down, like having a hot bath or going for a walk. For a Zen student, meditation is the basis of life. Whatever we are doing in the moment, whatever our circumstances, enlightenment can be realized. But it takes a lot of training. It takes regular practice. It takes diligent examination of our own minds.

Suggested Practice:
This Moment Is Exactly Right

Find a quiet place, direct your awareness to your breath, and each time something arises in your mind, notice and let it go. Do this for 20 minutes twice a day.

·········

It has taken me over 30 years of Zen training to truly realize that there is no such thing as "enlightenment." There is only living this life fully, being awake to its ultimate perfection – even if I'm caught up in political complaint. The way, and when I say "the way," I'm talking about this moment, right here, right now, at this typewriter, emotions from a heavily dreamed sleep whirling in body and mind, the pleasure in this sip of coffee. Enlightenment is not attainable – only pure awareness in this very moment is.

·········

I woke up this morning and realized my weekly commitment has been buried
  in snow.
Monkey mind took over, consuming me with questions.
Is there too much snow on the roof, can the deck hold this snow, what if it rains?
Can I shovel this – is the snow heavy or light?

The watery heavens have fallen into my lap, my life.
Swirling and twirling, floating across the lake the snow comes
Hiding the mountains, filling the streams.
The splendor and wonder are lost
Meditation surrenders to the mind's questions
I return to my seat
A little Buddha in a red cape and hat
and resume meditation.

Week 8

How Old Are We?

> Because mountains and waters have been active since before the Empty Eon, they are alive at this moment.

EARTH SCIENTISTS HAVE CONFIRMED in many ways that mountains and rivers are ancient. They have been on earth since long before there were human beings, plants, or animals. They go back many millions of years. When we are in the mountains or on the ocean, or sitting by a river as it flows by, we sense that we are communing with an ancestral form of existence. In the above sentence, Dogen is saying this, and something more. He's saying that even before there was a universe, even before anything at all existed, these mountains and rivers were alive.

So, what does he mean by that? How could that be? This goes back to a basic feeling that is at the heart of Asian cosmology. Contemporary cosmologists are now coming to the same conclusion – that is, to the idea that there is no beginning, that the idea of a beginning is a projection of a binary human mind, that the origin of the universe is more mysterious than anything our conceptual frameworks could possibly imagine.

When Dogen uses the phrase, "Empty Eon," he is referring to Buddhist cosmology where there are eons that succeed each other, one of which is an Empty Eon – a time when it appears that there is nothing. But even though it might it appear that in a given eon there is nothing, there is always this vital energy of movement, of impermanence. Impermanence is the only thing that is not impermanent. Impermanence is constant, as Dogen says, even when there is nothing.

I'm talking as if I know, but I don't know. I can't possibly know. All my thoughts, feelings, metaphors and ideas about impermanence are incorrect. Whatever I say is misleading. The whole idea of a beginning implies that there is an ending that is prior to beginning. But what's before that? Another beginning? And before that? Yet another beginning? It doesn't make sense. But it does make sense that there is only movement and that we exist here, now, in this moment, because that movement has never ceased. So, in some way we have always been here and will always be. We might lose our body; we will lose our body and the perceptions that depend on it. We will lose our memory and a coherent sense of an identity that depends on this body. But the vital energy that we are made of will not be lost. That part of us has always been and will always be.

Suggested Practice:
How Old Are We?

Try thinking about mountains and rivers as yourself and notice how everything becomes quite personal. What if you no longer identified with your body, your ideas, beliefs, possessions, nationality, gender, or family? What if, instead, you identified with the ongoing nature of living and dying? Think about this deeply. What would it mean to your daily life?

·········

I realized grace before I was born

The me that began with penetration
of poppa's sperm into momma's ovum
is just another spark of grace manifesting
as my body speech and mind
manifesting as mountains and waters.

Beneath decades of my delusions lay
the truth of grace's eternal presence
before and beyond body, speech & mind
before and beyond birth and death,
before and beyond mountains and waters.

Week 9

Bearing the Unbearable

SOON AFTER WE START a regular meditation practice, we realize that we are stuck in patterns. We suddenly become aware that objects, relationships and beliefs that we took for granted aren't solid. They just arise in awareness and, like everything else, dissolve away. At this point, mountains are mountains, in the narrow way. Then as our idea of a solid self stumbles until there is nobody there, mountains are not mountains any longer; rivers are not rivers. There is nothing to hang on to. We have stepped into an awake moment, and we have realized a deep truth about absolute reality.

This experience is both terrifying and freeing. When we reenter daily life after an experience like this, mountains are mountains and rivers are rivers once more. Everything is different; and nothing has changed. This coming back to ordinariness, this knowing that you can't hang on to ordinariness, brings awareness that our lives aren't ordinary at all. We begin to cultivate the realization of completion in every moment.

I've talked to many whose experience of their own or of a loved one's life-threatening illness has awakened them. It seems like we have to go through a horrible experience to find out that who we thought we are, we aren't, and that the self we want to hang on to can easily slip away. Learning this lack of solidity in our lives gives a completely different quality to what we know as ordinariness.

When we return to ordinary mind from a mind that has realized the truth of transience, delusion will still come up, although it is not as unconscious as it was before our realization. We still grasp after people, objects and experiences. We still compete with others; we still operate from gaining mind. For Dogen, it is sitting meditation that brings awareness that when a delusive thought arises, we are not that thought. Even with sustained practice, human foibles still arise, but we know what they are so now, we no longer identify with them, grasp after them, and insist on them. We recognize them as the root of suffering. It's easy to get lost and go down the road of suffering, but if we meditate, at some point we recognize what is actually happening.

"Oh, yes, that's right, suffering."

With Zen practice, there is a consolation that when profound reality – even if it is horrible profound reality – presents itself, there is a part of the mind that knows to say, "This is delusion, and it's passing. This doesn't have substance. Don't hang on to it."

Profound reality has no substance; it comes and goes. That's what makes it profound and that's how we bear the tremendous difficulties of a human lifetime. Horrible and unacceptable things happen to each and every one of us. There is no one who doesn't have to meet loss or a suffer a defeat that strikes us so hard we can't imagine how to live another day. This happens to every single person in a human lifetime and the way we bear that reality is by recognizing that it, too, is coming and going. What we are experiencing is not the absolute. That's how fully realizing impermanence helps us to bear the unbearable – even when it is very difficult.

Suggested Practice:
Bearing the Unbearable

If something happens that upsets you, step back from your emotions, turn your attention to your breath and remember that this will arise and pass, like everything else.

· · · · · · · ·

"This is a delusion, and it's passing. This doesn't have substance. Don't hang on to it."

Right, don't hang on, it will pass – the storms, the cold, the isolation – but what am I learning, how am I "being" in relation to these external challenges? I realize my lack of routine, discipline that keeps me centered as I watch the storms.

· · · · · · · ·

Stuck in patterns ... patterns created by networks of thought that are ultimately designed to ensure that I experience maximum pleasure, minimum pain in every moment.

Stuck in patterns ... patterns constructed and supported by a storehouse of impressions acquired since conception ... and perhaps before.

Stuck in patterns ... patterns of thought, speech and action, that repeat themselves over and over again, to reassure myself. 'I am real, I exist, I am important.'

Week 10

Drop the Bucket List

If we really enter this moment, and are truly here in our lives, we can be fully present with our experiences. But usually, we are not. If we look deeply into our own minds, it's shocking to realize that there is a constant undercurrent of desire and dissatisfaction. It's as if we are always searching for something. Identity and ego are a constant feature of our thinking. If we look past ideas about who we are and part the weeds of every thought to see what is behind each one, we find an expression of desire and self-interest. It's an ongoing thing that is always present. "I want to be kind; I want to be loved; I want to be justified; I want to be important: I want to be alive; I need this; I don't want that." All these things are constantly in our minds, even when we don't know they are there. Thoughts about self are, in fact, behind everything.

This means that as long as self-centred thoughts occupy any aspect of our consciousness we are not fully present. The underlying stream of desire causes us to see mountains and rivers in a two-dimensional way. And this underlying stream goes on all the time, even when we practice diligently. Self-centred concerns never go away completely. We need them to survive. But when we see through them and know them for what they are, we can be fully present, here, in this moment. And when we are fully present, each moment that manifests is the Buddha's expression of profound truth. As Dogen says, *Mountains and waters right now are the actualization of the buddhas and ancestors.*

The phrase, "right now" is actually the most significant phrase in this sentence. It has to do with the fact that this moment is not an isolated moment of time that passes away. It does pass away, but the energy that brings it forth has brought the previous moment forth and will bring the next moment forth. This energy is the energy of impermanence. It has always existed; it exists now, and it will always exist. Dogen is saying that every moment of passing time is, in itself, eternal.

And that's wonderful, because it means that you don't need to go anywhere. Most of us like the idea of a bucket list. I always wanted to do this; I have to do that before I die or my life won't be complete. But according to this teaching, even if you never left your room you would be everywhere, and you would be able to participate fully with everything, because every moment is complete. That is the profound truth of this teaching.

Suggested Practice:
Drop the Bucket List

If you have a bucket list of things you are hoping to do before you die, notice how often it seduces you away from present moment awareness.

·········

I don't have a written bucket list of places or things that distract me; I think these will unfold.... I know the time in front of me is shorter than the time behind and I feel so compelled not to waste it (the time). At the same moment, I know that I do waste most of my time by not simply being present.

When I am in nature – walking in a forest, picking raspberries, lying on the earth, walking by the water, I don't think of time or presence, I simply am. Living indoors this winter has made me so aware of my deep connections to the life around me because I am not out there – I am looking through a window.

Then it happens, the sun reflects off the snow filling me with light and in that I am no longer "waiting" for spring, I am allowing spring to blossom inside of me – one moment at a time.

The moment passes. I carry the light to the kitchen and wash dishes.

Week 11

Being Fully Alive

Because mountains and rivers have been active since before the Empty Eon, they are alive at this moment. Because they have been the self since before form arose, they are emancipation and realization.

These two sentences are parallel expressions. The first one is about time; the second one is about space and matter that exists in space. Dogen is saying that mountains and rivers have always existed. They transcend time, and when they do appear in time, they are all-inclusive.

And this is true for us humans as well. We are much bigger than we think we are. The essence of what we *actually* are existed before any other entity ever existed, and because of that, our selfness, our selfhood, like the selfness and selfhood of mountains and waters, is its own liberation, our own unique expression of absolute reality. In other words, we, like mountains and rivers, are not as limited as we appear to be. This is exactly the heart of Zen teaching. Like time and space, we have no boundaries. Our only boundaries are falsely created by beliefs and self-centred thinking that result from societal and cultural conditioning.

So often we make the mistake of thinking that this moment isn't really all that important. But for Dogen, all of time is here, right now. Everything is complete in this moment. This little life, this little person that comes and goes so quickly, and is able to accomplish so little between birth and death, contains everything in the entire universe. All of space and time is right here in the destiny of this one life. That is Dogen's astounding statement.

It's hard to feel this in the nitty gritty of the daily grind, but when we go into the mountains, we feel it. This is why most of us love to go into the mountains. If we lace up our hiking boots, strap on a backpack with food and tent, and walk for two or three days on a mountain trail, we will eventually feel this union with all of time and space.

The Chinese people knew this. The monks in China would walk many hundreds of miles and travel from one monastery to another. They never followed, like in the Christian monastic tradition, the practice of staying cloistered in one monastery. Chinese Chan (Zen) monks believed that religious practice is a life of wandering in the mountains. They would enroll in one monastery, stay for a few years for basic training, and then go walking in the mountains for months at a time. Some lived in isolated mountain hermitages for decades.

Suggested Practice:
Being Fully Alive

Take some time to walk in the mountains. Learn about the hiking groups in your area and join them on a mountain hike. While there, separate from the chatter and bring your awareness to the feeling of boundlessness of the mountains, the rivers and of your own life.

· · · · · · · · ·

    Monarch Mountains rise above my horizon.
    Six inches of snow fell in the night
    Eternally they hold the lake of ancient glaciers
    Temporal snow waxes and wanes
    Sun shines
    Spring is promised
    I walk the mountains in my mind
    In summer, I'll return
    Listening to the snowy water flow
    back into the glacial lake.

Week 12

The Green Mountains Are Always Walking

> The green mountains are always walking; a stone woman gives birth to
> a child at night.

WHEN YOU MEDITATE, you sit still, feel your breath and enter the immediacy of being fully alive, right here, right now. Thoughts will come and go. It could be about something you have forgotten to do, or a thought about a problem or project in your life. Whatever it is, it comes and it goes. It's the same as breathing – it just comes and goes like a melody in the heart. In meditation, we eventually realize that all our concepts, all our beliefs are just that, concepts and beliefs. We don't have to attach to them; we don't have to believe in them.

We think the mountains are solid. We think our concepts are solid. They're not. They exist in this moment and then they are gone. When we realize this, we know that mountains are walking. There is no such thing as something solid; everything is moving all the time.

A stone woman gives birth to a child at night. This is the mysterious birth before the universe formed. It is the birth that never ends and never begins. All of reality is like this. This Zen saying expresses what Dogen is trying to express in *Mountains and Rivers Sutra*. In emptiness and in awareness, everything comes and goes; everything is born and dies. A stone woman, by any definition cannot give birth. But in this sentence, she gives birth at night. This is Dogen's way of saying that true birth, the birth that makes all birth possible, is always going on beyond the world we can see.

We need our usual ideas about who we are and what we think this world is for practical purposes. We need to communicate with each other to manage daily life, but if that's all we have, if we don't see that all things come and go, we will suffer and we will make others suffer.

We all know we are going to die, and we all struggle for understanding and meaning in human life. We look for meaning in order to make peace with life. That's why there are religions. Religion is a struggle to give meaning to life and death.

> The green mountains are always walking. A stone woman gives birth to
> a child at night.

These phrases, *The green mountains are always walking* and *The stone woman gives birth to child at night*, express everything that Dogen is trying to convey about the reality of human life.

Suggested Practice:
The Green Mountains Are Always Walking

Memorize one of these phrases. Say it to yourself over and over for the next week as you sit, walk, work, eat and fall asleep. Breathe with it and stay with it. You might feel something in your living as a result of staying with the phrase. You might feel your place in this constant motion.

· · · · · · · ·

I am a green mountain
walking in an ever-deepening spiral
into inconceivable mysterious birth
before the universe was born
and long after it has died.

I am a child born at night
from the cold hard womb
of a stone woman,
born as a mountain
where I am embraced and
nourished by a soft forest floor
watered by spring and fall rains
caressed by a passing breeze.
I am a melody in your heart
here and gone, here and gone
here and gone

Week 13

The Paradox of Zen

For the last three or four weeks, I've been presenting some pretty profound ideas about what life actually is, and I'm thinking that some could be feeling perplexed. I've been explicating the first paragraph in 13th Century Zen Master Dogen's essay, *Mountains and Rivers Sutra*, where he lays out his vision of reality. Dogen was a well-intentioned philosopher, poet and spiritual teacher. He wrote this essay to help us awaken from the dream of self-centredness and see a vision of reality that can free us from suffering. But the real question is, "How can I let this vision inform my daily life?"

The answer is easy. "Meditate in the morning, walk mindfully, be of service to others, eat your lunch, do the dishes, take a rest, meditate in the evening, be helpful, laugh when something is funny, cry when it's sad, take a bath, get dressed, have children, see them grow up, see them have children, watch them grow up, die. In other words, live an ordinary life but with extraordinary awareness.

To ask, "How can I let this vision inform my life?" is to ask a great question because all the activities that I just described are, in a way, not about doing anything special. We usually think that "doing something" means to get it done, to fix something, to make something different from what it is. We so often operate on the assumption that something is wrong with our lives, that we need to do something about us. But what I just described is nothing more than a simple life lived moment-by-moment, without stress.

But there is a paradox here. In order to reach this stress-free state, we have to struggle to drop our conditioned views. We have been conditioned to think that as humans, we have to fix something, master something, or accomplish something. This conditioning, that something is essentially wrong with us, is very deep, but if we want to live the Zen life, we have to drop that idea.

So, on the one hand, Zen practice is easy. In fact, it is the easiest thing in the world. Once we have let go of our conditioning, practice is satisfying and effortless. But we have to make a huge effort to reach the place where we can appreciate our lives on that level. Reading and studying the profound teachings of Zen Master Dogen is interesting, but the only way to truly understand those teachings is to live them. It takes discipline, effort and a regular meditation practice.

Suggested Practice:
The Paradox of Zen

Set up a place in your home where you can begin a regular meditation practice. First thing in the morning and last thing before you go to bed, meditate for twenty minutes. To ensure that your meditation practice is as effective as it could be, meditate with others at a zendo at least once a week to hear the teachings. Make every activity in your daily life a meditation practice.

·········

Dogen's Koan #26
The National Teacher's "Pure Dharma Body"

Main Case
Zen Master Huizhong of Nanyang was asked by Emperor Suzong of the Tang Dynasty, "What is the Samadhi of no conflict?"
Nanyang said, "Your Majesty, go trample on Vairocana's head."
Emperor Su said, "I don't understand."
Nanyang said, "Don't regard the self as the pure dharma body."

·········

Oh ... I get it. It's not all about me.

Week 14

We Are Awesome

Before continuing with our study of the 13th Century text, *Mountains and Rivers Sutra*, I want to talk about the main reason Dogen's essay seems so difficult and obscure.

We in the west have been educated in a particular way, and because of that, when we look at Dogen's writing we naturally try to understand it as we would any other text that we have read in high school or college. But Dogen is not writing this essay so we can say what it means on an exam, employ it in conversation, or apply it in activity and work. This is how we usually think about spiritual writings. Dogen's way is not like that. Reading and studying Dogen's writing has a very different purpose than the purpose that underlies most spiritual writings. To understand Dogen, we have to enter into a bigger mind, and Dogen's main purpose is to give us access to this greater mind.

This is very difficult: difficult to enter and difficult to sustain. Even if you periodically enter that bigger mind, your thinking will eventually return to the same mindset you have always had. We all do this. I've often come up against a phrase like, *The green mountains are always walking* with my usual mindset. It's at those times that I believe that I'll never be able to appreciate Dogen's writing. He just doesn't make sense. "Mountains don't walk!" I say. "What is he talking about?" I just don't get it.

But of course, I can't understand what Dogen means by "Green mountains are always walking" from my usual mindset, because Dogen's essay is all about undoing that mindset. Unlike much of the writing I'm accustomed to, it is not about adding to what I already know; it's about undoing the teaching that has resulted in my ordinary western-trained mind. Dogen's purpose here to undo everything that I have learned that ties me up in the knots that have caused me to live in ways that are harmful to me, to my close relations and even to this planet. His purpose is to undo all that and show me how to live just as I am – a sacred, awesome presence in this moment of time on this miniscule spot of space. In other words, he is trying to show me how to stop confusing myself with my thoughts. That's why his writing can be so perplexing.

Suggested Practice:
We Are Awesome

Before you head out into your day, take some time to meditate deeply on the miracle of the simple fact that you are here, in this place, at this time. Making a gratitude list can help evoke this state of mind. When you have established a sense of appreciation for your life, begin your day's activity. Then, as you go through the day, notice, without judging, how often you lose that appreciation.

· · · · · · · ·

I have spent the last two days driving; moving from a Spring that is in full bloom in the south back to one that is just waking up in the North. It is like my life moving from one state of full-bloom awareness to the realization that I have once again fallen asleep.

Sharing this practice with you every week is a touchstone to the greater sense of being, remembering the mystery, contemplating the unanswerable questions, appreciating that in this moment, I am alive.

Week 15

Beyond Common Sense

IN THE NEXT SECTION of his essay, *Mountains and Rivers Sutra,* Dogen refers to koans, or traditional Zen stories that appear nonsensical. In all of his writing, Dogen's main purpose is to be helpful. Koans such as "green mountains are always walking," are helpful because they are companions on the path that continually remind us that we are awesome, just as we are. We don't have to do anything to be awesome. Because we can't use ordinary logic to figure out koans, they break us out of habitual mind. You can be stuck in an old way of thinking and they will suddenly pop, unbidden, into awareness as a reminder of how awesome this life actually is.

Koans present only a fragment of reality, and if we let go of our tendency to make sense of everything, the koan imagery can break us out of our ordinary idea of time. This is crucial, because otherwise, we have no answer to anyone in deep despair, or who is dying, because despair and death just don't make sense. To understand these facts of life, you have to step into the realm that is beyond common sense, into the realm of the impossible. And Dogen, as well as the koans, invite us to see that the impossible is possible.

Buddha was faced with the same problem as Dogen. He considered the suffering that comes from old age, disease and death, realized a way to transcend it, and then wondered how he could express the full significance of his realization. He decided that explanations wouldn't cut it, so he developed teachings that help us make sense of old age, disease and death, and he taught practices that could lead us to reducing suffering and increasing happiness. Any one of us can study his teachings and try to put them into practice. But when we do that, we enter a process that will lead us to full realization of enlightenment, which is also the realization that, at depth, our human life is unexplainable.

The ancient Zen koans and Dogen's essay, *Mountains and Rivers Sutra* are not simply attempts to explain the unexplainable. This is why we can't penetrate their meaning with ordinary thinking. These writings are an attempt to help us enter enlightened mind, that is, a state of mind that transcends ordinary thinking, so we can experience a brief moment of freedom from seeing the world though our own desires and opinions.

We naturally think that everything has to make sense. The reality expressed in koans and in Dogen's writing help us reach a stage where things don't have to make sense in an ordinary way. Only then does the depth of life and death make real sense; a sense that includes, and yet, is beyond, common sense.

Suggested Practice:
Beyond Common Sense

Memorize the phrase "green (or blue) mountains are always walking" and, during your day, repeat it silently to yourself as you would a mantra. Notice what kinds of understanding and inner experience this practice evokes.

· · · · · · · · ·

the stone woman gives birth
to the creatures of the night
to silence and stars
to refreshing sleep
a new dawn

· · · · · · · · ·

There is only one thing that truly makes sense to me.
Zen training is endless and it includes everything.

Week 16

Study This Deeply

Now, I'm going to examine, in more detail, the first half of the koan that Dogen quotes in his essay, *Mountains and Rivers Sutra*. He writes that

> the green mountains are always walking; a stone woman gives birth to a child at night.

In discussing this koan, Dogen also says, *Mountains do not lack the characteristics of mountains*. That is, mountains are mountains because they do the things mountains do, and possess the characteristics that mountains possess. We call it a 'mountain' because it's tall and it's made of certain elements.

But Dogen is not just talking about mountains. For Dogen, mountains represent everything. What he says about mountains is true for humans as well. We are full of the characteristics that make us who we are. No one else has our characteristics. Because of this uniqueness, your life is like no other life that has ever existed or will ever exist. Dogen adds that *mountains always abide in ease and always walk*. Like us, they are both profoundly at rest and are always walking. That's what existence is. Existence means you are always profoundly at rest and you are always in movement. Then he says we should *examine in detail the characteristics of mountains walking*.

He is telling us to examine in detail the characteristics of our lives. We do this when sitting in meditation. How many of us would agree that we have characteristics we are not thrilled with, that we think should be different? Most of us feel we could improve aspects of our physical appearance, our psychological makeup, and our habits. But Dogen says no; don't improve your characteristics. It's your characteristics that make you a unique aspect of existence. And that existence is profoundly settled and at rest, and it is also in constant motion.

Just study how this is true. Don't try to evaluate, plan and strive to change your life. Just study it at ever deeper levels and see how in every moment you are both at rest and in motion. Change is going on all the time.

We think mountains don't walk because it seems that, on the surface, they aren't doing what human beings do. But they are walking. They, like us, are always coming from stillness to activity, always changing. Rocks roll down the sides of mountains, water changes its size and shape. With shifting tectonic plates, mountains literally move from one place to another.

For us and for mountains, every moment is a moment of activity: the mind's activity, the heart's activity, the soul's activity, the body's activity. Even when we sit still in zazen, our blood is racing, cells are being sluffed off, our nerves are firing. For Dogen, that is how we walk, and that is how mountains walk. So, don't doubt that mountains walk. Dogen concludes by encouraging us to penetrate these words, to study them and understand them deeply.

Suggested Practice:
Study This Deeply

Each time you notice yourself criticizing one of your characteristics and wishing you could change, remind yourself that you are always changing, that you don't need to force change. Relax into rest and allow the change to take place. The mountain will transform in its own time.

· · · · · · · · ·

"abide in ease and always walk."

My early morning walk through the garden.
Peas ok? Check. Lettuce ok? Check.
Are the slugs attacking my sweet pea towers?
So many plant babies in my tender care
Each one abiding in ease and always walking.

Week 17

This Too Will Change

Because green mountains walk, they are permanent.

THE WORD PERMANENT might be misleading because there is only one thing that is permanent – impermanence. When people say, "I don't trust him or her," I answer, "You can absolutely trust them. You can trust them to be themselves." Similarly, you can trust impermanence to be constant; it is the one thing that you *can* trust. Things come and go; you can trust that, always.

And ironically, there is salvation in that. If things are really bad they won't last, so don't worry. If things are really good, they won't get boring, so don't worry. Nothing stays the same. And that's a good thing, because if something that is really good stayed that way, it would soon turn out to be really bad. It's good because it's impermanent.

For example, your son's first wedding is not every day. That's why it's so great. Imagine if your son's first wedding were every single day. Every day you would have to deal with all those relatives, all the champagne, all the food. It would soon get tiring. But because your son's first wedding is only once, and because it will be over at the end of the day, it is truly wonderful.

So that's what Dogen is saying here. Because the green mountains are constantly walking, they are truly constant. This quality of constancy is one of the greatest virtues of Zen training. That's why exciting people and people who love excitement don't usually stick with Zen practice. Zen virtue is not brilliant. It's not a flashy enlightenment experience. In Zen training, we don't try to achieve great heights, because if we achieve great heights, we miss our life as it is. The great height is to be alive together in this world. There is nothing beyond this. So, to strive for a fantastic enlightenment experience is to miss the awesome presence of your life as it is, here in this moment.

True Zen practice is the constancy of showing up, of being there, of bringing your whole heart to every moment of your life, whether in the zendo or on the fifth day of a retreat, whether you are cleaning garbage on the street as a community service or wiping peanut butter off your kitchen countertop. Zen virtue is the constancy of putting yourself right in the middle of the walking mountains, of the ever-changing reality of moment to moment living.

Suggested Practice:
This Too Will Change

Take some time to notice where you are operating on the assumption that something – bad health, good health, abundance, poverty, happiness or unhappiness – will always be present. Remind yourself that this too will change.

Week 18

A Mountain Meditation

This week I am asking you to do a guided mountain meditation that may help you penetrate the essence of what Dogen means with the words, *the green mountains are constantly walking*. This meditation is normally done in a sitting position. Begin by sensing the support you feel from your chair or cushion. Find a position of stability and poise, upper body balanced over your hips, shoulders in a comfortable but alert posture, hands on your lap or knees, arms hanging by their own weight, like heavy curtains, stable and relaxed.

When you are ready, bring awareness to your breath, the actual physical sensations of breath, feeling each breath lift and relax your belly as the air comes in and goes out. When the mind stabilizes even a little, allow an image of a mountain you have known form in your mind. Feel its overall shape, its peaks, it's sloping sides, its base rooted in the bedrock of the earth's crust.

Now, imagine, if you will, that you are that mountain. Let your head become the peak supported by the rest of your body and affording a panoramic view. Let your shoulders and arms become the sides of the mountain. Your buttocks and legs become the solid base. With each breath, become that breathing mountain, alive and vital, yet unwavering in inner stillness, beyond words and thought, a centered, grounded, presence.

As you sit, become aware that as the sun walks across the mountain, light and shadows constantly change and move in the mountain's stillness. Your surface teems with life and activity – streams flow, snow melts, night follows day, day follows night. Through it all, you, the mountain, sit still, experiencing change in each moment, aware that you are constantly changing, yet always just being yourself.

In any season, you may find yourself enshrouded in clouds, visited by violent storms, buffeted by snow and wind. But through it all, the mountain sits. When snow falls, the mountain is there. When the snow melts and there is furious water flowing downwards making great gouges out of the mountain's sides, the mountain is still there. Through blistering summer heat, it is there. Lightning strikes the top, it is there. It's been there for thousands of years. It will be there for the next thousand years.

Dogen says that *because the green mountains constantly walk, they are constant*. What is more constant than a mountain? A mountain is the very image of constancy and yet, the mountains are constantly walking. Everything in the mountain is always, literally, changing. We now know that every atom on that mountain is in motion. The mountain is walking, in constant motion, and yet it is constant in its impermanence.

Suggested Practice:
A Mountain Meditation

Take some time to record this meditation or memorize it; and then during the day go to a place where you will not be interrupted, find a comfortable sitting posture and either listen to the recording or silently recite it from memory.

. . . .

> Last week the daffodils faded and the tulips came
> The lupine and chives and irises will soon turn
> my world purple along with the lilacs.
>
> I relish the sun, the garden, the change in season
> and tonight, I experience the changes within myself
> as I have not been moderate – gobbling up the sunshine,
> not paying attention to a body that was asking for a rest
> but this will all pass in the night – the stone woman will
> give birth to a new day and the primroses will open
> once again to the sun.

. . . .

> I spent a morning on a high alpine ridge looking out on the Canadian Rockies, doing qigong, zazen and being the mountain, when, suddenly, in my final standing qigong, out of the forest a mature doe climbed onto the ridge, close enough that I could have reached out to touch her as she passed. She paid me no mind, viewed me as just another aspect of mountain. In this body, I am just another piece of mountain life – no more important, no less important, than the tiny red-leafed plants growing through the crust of snow.

Week 19

We Are All the Same

I suggested you do a mountain meditation to deepen your understanding of what Zen Master Dogen meant when he said that the green mountains are constantly walking. Now, I am moving on to the next sentence in Dogen's essay, *Mountains and Rivers Sutra*. He writes that

> although mountains walk more swiftly than the wind, someone in the mountains does not realize or understand it.

We are all in the mountains. That is, we are all in impermanence, because we all exist. We are all "in being." The pervasiveness of human misunderstanding is amazing to me. Men don't understand women; Americans don't understand Europeans; Israelis don't understand Palestinians. All these misunderstandings are so consequential. They result in broken families, wars of words, and even in wars where powerful weapons destroy whole communities of people.

But from the standpoint of what Dogen is saying here, it is unbelievable that we do not understand, absolutely love and depend on each other because we are all the same. We all exist as the same mountain. When we think about that, how can we not embrace each other? We share so much simply because we all exist here together. We have the same problems; we know the same things; we don't know the same things. We have the same suffering as all other people and cultures who share this mountain. We even have the same suffering as the trees and the foxes. We each need to find food and shelter. We all need connection and love. We all face illness, aging and death. How do we not look at one another and burst out with tears of gratitude that we are not alone here? We have each other. How wonderful!

And yet, there are all these misunderstandings. It's quite tragic, isn't it?

So Dogen says that we are all in the mountains, but when we are in the mountains we don't know or understand how the mountains are changing or moving all the time, and how, at the same time, they are constant.

Why don't we understand this? We don't understand this because we are the mountain. We can only truly understand something from the outside. This is why Dogen, in another essay in which he teaches the practice of meditation, tells us to "take the step backwards" and shine the light of awareness on the reality of our lives. When we take that step backwards, we can see that we all live on the same mountain and that if I harm you, I am harming myself. We can see that the mountain, that is, that our life, is walking more swiftly than the wind.

Suggested Practice:
We Are All the Same

The next time you are in a disturbed state about something that another person or group of people has or has not done, take that step backwards and remind yourself that we all share the same suffering and we all want to find and realize freedom from that suffering.

· · · · · · · ·

Congratulations to us for keeping on going. I just want to say that in some ways, this practice is like zazen. We sit and sit and sit until the same old thoughts get tired of coming and going and then, "Boom!" Suddenly we are in a whole new territory of consciousness – the repetition has gone and we are, still anchored to our seat, gone, gone, gone, beyond and at the same time, totally present.

· · · · · · · ·

I am just like that – the person in front of me in line who can't seem to find a credit card that works,
the man next door who decides to mow his lawn on Sunday at 7 am,
the woman trying to console a crying baby,
the lovers kissing goodbye at the airport, not wanting to let go of each other,
the little girl picking wildflowers for her mom who is sitting in a wheelchair,
I am that. I am all of that.

Week 20

Every Birth Is a Miracle

'In the mountains' means the blossoming of the entire world.

THIS PHRASE THAT DOGEN USES, "the blossoming of the entire world," comes from a poem that Prajnatara, a 6th Century Indian monk, wrote for his student, Bodhidharma, who was the first Zen teacher in China. Prajnatara's poem goes like this.

> From the mind-ground, seeds sprout;
> Reality appears in all its forms.
> It grows until the fruit is full, and enlightenment is complete.
> The flower opens and the whole world arises.

This poem expresses a basic teaching from Buddhist mind-only philosophy in which there is no fundamental difference between consciousness and matter. Matter is a form of consciousness. Consciousness produces matter. That's why, by entering fully into our own human consciousness, we can embrace and understand all of space and time. Through Zen practice, we can rest deeply in consciousness and realize that each detail of our lives is a full expression of that greater consciousness. This is true for all of creation; it is as true for a rock or a plant as it is for a human being. Everything is included in consciousness. That's why Dogen says that a flower blossoms and the whole world opens up.

Anyone who has witnessed a human birth understands this. You could say, "Well, there's too many people on the earth, so what's the big deal about another birth?" But that's not what we feel. Instead we feel that the whole world is different now; this is a miracle. The feeling is universal and unmistakable. At that moment of birth, even though birth is not unusual, we marvel at it and feel hope for the whole world. That's what Dogen means when he says that *in the mountains means the blossoming of the entire world*. Reality is reborn with every flower that blooms.

But in our ordinary daily lives, we somehow place ourselves outside of this reality and don't really know or understand the mystery of our own existence. There are two kinds of not-understanding. In one kind, you are in the middle of your life, and you really appreciate your life with all its joys and sorrows. You live fully and know that you are connected to everyone and everything, even though you don't really understand how, and you know you never will understand. That's one kind of not-understanding.

The other kind of not-understanding makes us grumpy and brings suffering. With this kind of not-understanding, we make everyone around us suffer as well, and we can't accept our lack of understanding. We think we should understand; we think that someone else does understand. So, we make up stories that give us the illusion of understanding. Most world religions are based on these stories.

Suggested Practice:
Every Birth Is a Miracle

Take some time to reflect on how much you don't understand about the miracle of life. How much of what you think you understand is based on old stories that others have told you? In this way, fully enter the mystery of "not-understanding."

· · · · · · · ·

    I know the feeling of waking in the forest, surrounded by life I cannot see – the whole organism of life that lies under me, the sound of the birds above, the rain that is misting over the trees.
    I know the amazing gift of conceiving and giving birth. I watch the bees pollinating the flowers, the worm moving across the grass, guardians of life on earth. But "knowing" and "understanding" the miracle are two different things....
    How is it possible that I am alive, sitting in this space, listening to the birds and trying to answer this question?

Week 21

All Beings Are Precious

THE WHOLE POINT of Zen practice is to teach us that we are not separate from anything. Thirteenth Century Zen Master Dogen expressed this in his *Mountains and Rivers Sutra*.

> If you doubt mountains walking, you don't know your own walking. It's not that you are not walking; it's just that you don't know or understand your own walking. If you want to know your own walking you should fully know the green mountains walking.

Until you appreciate and fully embrace the mystery of mountains walking, you haven't really seen your own life, and you don't appreciate the enormous measure of who and what you are.

Often, as we get older, we do appreciate this amazing opportunity of human life. I've heard many seniors lament the stupid things they did, the time they wasted. But of course, at the time, they had no idea what they were doing, and, in some way, what happened in their lives is exactly what had to happen. Dogen is saying that we don't know our own life until we know constancy, impermanence and letting go of the self-centred view. The big pattern, which includes constant walking and complete rest, characterizes all existence, and until we have contemplated our own constant walking and complete rest through zazen and spiritual practice, we won't fully appreciate our own life.

Dogen goes on to say

> Green mountains are neither sentient nor insentient; and you are neither sentient nor insentient.

This statement is kind of surprising because we think that we are sentient and mountains are not. Dogen's words may express the essential difference between Western and Abrahamic religions and Far East Asian Buddhism. In western thought, there is a hierarchy of beings. The highest beings are invisible, and of the visible beings, humans are highest. Creatures that we think have less capacity are lower beings, and objects without life are lower still. You can't kill people; but you can kill animals. And it doesn't matter if you trash stuff that isn't alive, because it is a lower order of being.

Throughout history, we have imposed this hierarchy on humans as well. During colonization, Africans and North American Indians could be bought and sold or killed. The Nazis considered Jews to be a disposable race, and to radicals in the Middle East and Africa, infidels are so low on the hierarchy that it's a spiritual act to kill them. The examples are endless. At the same time, there are human beings who are so precious that if you insult them you must be killed, or if you deny them as the highest beings, you burn in a lake of fire for eternity.

For Dogen, all beings are equally important. He often says that even roof tiles, walls and pebbles are sentient beings and they all express the teaching of compassion.

Suggested Practice:
All Beings Are Precious

Try treating every person, animal and object in your world as though they are equally precious and see how this affects the way you feel about your life.

·········

I have a garden dedicated to bees, butterflies and hummingbirds,
I have a bee house for mason bees.
The yard is full of flowers and lovely beings.
In the back I have a deck. The wasps love this deck and build nests underneath,
They are happy, I am not,
I end up putting out wasp traps, killing hundreds of wasps over the summer.
I like to think of myself as living in harmony with all beings
In the summer I know I am at the top of the order, deciding who will live and who will die.
It is a very humbling and shameful feeling
so when a wasp comes in the house, I capture him
throw him out giving him a chance.

·········

I am aware that, by putting those pea plants on the front line to attract the slugs to the poison I laid out, I am like a general who sends the infantry out of the trenches and into the gunfire of battle, knowing they will be maimed or killed. And indeed, those warrior plants are chewed and dying while the ones I'm growing for me are flourishing. It isn't easy to be only good and kind to all beings when you are a gardener. This is the wonderful training of gardening.

Week 22

The Wisdom of Our Bodies

DOGEN SAYS that mountains are both sentient and insentient. They are insentient in the sense that they are physical presences without consciousness. But of course, mountains are expressive. When we study a mountain, we feel something special. We feel what the mountain expresses. An earth without mountains is a different earth, and when you live in mountain country you have a special feeling about the mountains. They affect you. Similarly, if you live in another kind of country, such as the prairies, the big sky is very different from mountains and expresses something different about life and about human consciousness. So, mountains are insentient. They are just stuff; but they are also sentient in that they express something.

We humans are the same as mountains. We are insentient in that we are just stuff. There is not much difference between this body and a mountain. If we analyze the materials in both we see that they are more or less the same stuff. But our stuff is so smart. It regulates the heart, makes sure we breathe, maintains homeostasis. Our bodies are enormously complex and intelligent. In that sense, our bodies, like the mountains, are so wise and powerful that without saying a word we express something meaningful. Language has words that combine together to make meaning. People are like words, in that they too combine together to make meaning. This is how meaning appears; it is created among us.

In Zen meditation and practice we emphasize the body. We use our capacity for awareness to feel the body, to connect to the breath. We allow the body to be as it is, in the moment. In so doing, we unite our consciousness with the universal experience of being a body. This is one of the most important parts of zen meditation, because we so often mistakenly think of the body as a container for something else that is the "real" us. Our culture and our conditioning have not taught us to appreciate the wisdom of the body, or, for that matter, the wisdom of the mountain and the prairies.

Our human body is like the ocean that has the profound wisdom to be in tune with the moon, to be in tune with the spinning of the earth, to be a perfect habitat for ocean creatures. How did this happen? How did the ocean become so perfect for ocean creatures? How did the mountains become so perfect for mountain creatures? It's amazing!

We human beings are the same. Our bodies are perfectly adapted to this planet, to the food that's available, to air and water, to the consciousness that we possess. Our bodies, exactly as we are, are as perfect and as wise as the insentience of the mountains, the prairies and the ocean.

Suggested Practice:
The Wisdom of Our Bodies

Intentionally rest your awareness on the experience of being a body.

· · · · · · · ·

Letter from my body.

First I want to tell you how grateful I am that you helped me burn off 60 pounds over the last year and a half. I can't begin to express the difference it has made.

Yesterday, when Jake was pruning the temple's plum trees, I noticed that instead of hobbling and wobbling to get a tool he needed, I was running and leaping through the garden – which made me giggle – so, actually, I was running and leaping and giggling through the garden. I thought I'd never be able to run and leap again.

· · · · · · · ·

Sensations, impressions, interpretations, pain, pleasure, awe, intelligence understanding, intuition, the passing of time as wrinkles, the glory of love, the possibilities of discovery, the changing color of my hair, the story of my life emerging anew every day. My body, my life.

Week 23

Blue Mountains Walking

WE HAVE TALKED about the insentience of human beings. But of course, we are also sentient; we sense, feel and express. The word "sentient," at its roots, means "to go in feeling." Conventionally we say that something without thought is insentient. Rocks aren't sentient, but what about plants? They adjust and move with conditions. Does that mean they are sentient?

Dogen says that everything is both sentient and insentient. To appreciate that about ourselves is crucial to our balance and health, and when we understand what he is actually saying, we will not doubt that mountains are both sentient and insentient or that they are always walking. When we fully enter the mountains, and stay long enough to shake off daily life, we feel this walking. We feel that we and the mountains know each other. When we fully enter the mountains something magical happens, and we no longer doubt that the mountains are alive and moving.

Dogen says that

> we should study the mountains using numerous worlds as our standards.

He is saying that there is no end to studying mountains. And this is true of us humans too. It is so fascinating to be alive. We can meditate forever and realize so much about our life. But then we get up and go into the world to meet just one person. How much do we know about that one person? Hang around that person long enough and we can learn everything there is to know about human beings. We could study philosophy and never finish learning about it. And even if you read all the philosophers, you have only read them in English. Why don't you take up the German philosophers? What we can understand about being alive is infinite. For example, I've been studying Buddhism for close to 50 years, and I know just a little. For one thing, hardly any teachings have been translated into English, and I don't read Asian languages. It's staggering to realize how much more there is to know. Research biologists can spend an entire life studying one insect and still feel they have only scratched the surface.

Anywhere you turn you will find something that is absolutely worth knowing. And everything is telling us something about life and all its colour and beauty, all its creativity and destructiveness. Dogen is saying that we can never finish appreciating this phenomenal world. On the one hand, he says, we don't need to get up from our meditation cushion. We could sit for the rest of our lives, and everything is right there. But when we do get up from our cushions, whatever we encounter in this life is our life and is also, completely interesting, mysterious and amazing. Whatever spiritual path we take up, we can realize this truth because everything is a study of the mountains walking.

Suggested Practice:
Blue Mountains Walking

Take some time to study the piece of ground under your feet. How did the pebbles and dirt form? What ancient earth process left them where they are? What are the plants saying?

• • • • • • • •

I live at the bottom of a glacier, miles of ice and water above me. Glacier is gone, I am here, tilling the rocky bottom, rich in minerals blueberries, raspberries, strawberries, growing everywhere. I add water, the earth adds the sun. I walk the rocky soil waiting for the abundance to deliver itself. My feet touch the earth, my tongue tastes the sun, the minerals the delicate juice of the berries as they celebrate another year of life.

• • • • • • • •

The piece of ground under my feet.

Standing on a gravel patch in the zen garden, knowing what is beneath my feet – gravel, landscape fabric, clay, bedrock, and down to the molten core of earth whirling me around its axis through endless space and time. The pebbles, purchased from a Kootenay Lake gravel pit, developed through water erosion after glaciers carved this valley between the Selkirks and the Purcells. The piece of ground under my feet contains this valley and its peoples. Will the pebbles tell me their story?

Week 24

Take the Backward Step

> Clearly examine the blue mountains walking and examine your own walking. Examine backward walking and investigate the fact that walking forward goes on all the time.

In another essay which teaches us how to meditate, Dogen says that the backward step is the heart of zazen. In explaining how to meditate, he says, "Take the backward step and turn the light inward. Your body-mind, of itself, will drop off, and original enlightenment will appear. If you want to realize enlightenment, take this step backwards."

When we sit in zazen, we examine our consciousness very carefully. This requires a certain amount of concentration because if our mind is distracted, there is no way we can see what is going on in awareness. But if we sit quietly so there is not so much thinking going on, and if we refrain from chasing thinking, thoughts will come and go more slowly because the mind is calm. Then it may occur to us to wonder: where does *that* thought come from; or we might question *how* it appeared there all of a sudden.

But if our mind is racing, that question never occurs to us because we are too busy thinking about stuff. And really, isn't it true that mostly we think about a projected idea of ourselves? Even when relaxing in our living room the mind is directed outward. Indeed, *most* of our thinking is directed outward. The mind is always pursuing something. For example, people often think about the future. "Tomorrow I'm going to do this or that." But if I'm thinking about tomorrow, I'm only thinking about a projected idea of myself. Others think about the past. But if I'm mad at myself over what a stupid thing I did yesterday, or congratulating myself on something I did well, I'm not really thinking about my true self. I'm still thinking about a projected idea of self. Dogen says that thinking about a projected self is taking a forward step. It is the mind leaving this very moment in time and space. It is not thinking about our true self, the self that exists here and now. We all know how to take the forward step. We do it all the time.

But Dogen is telling us to take the backward step, to stop thinking about stuff and to go back to the source of thinking. He is telling us to shine the light inward, and if we notice ourselves heading into the past or the future, to step back into our lives, as they are, in this moment. We do this over and over in zazen, but he tells us to do that over and over again whether we are meditating, gardening or in a conversation.

Suggested Practice:
Take the Backward Step

Take twenty minutes each day to sit still, and notice whether your thoughts take you into the future or the past. The moment you notice, let go of that projection, take the backward step, and shine the light inward.

·········

Feeding the Enemy

    I've placed signage on my way through
    The dark clinging vines of obesity
    I began with seeing how wrong
    I have been, how wrong we have all been
    about intentional fat loss. We thought we
    could think our way through it.
    But now I know for sure; my brain is NOT in control
    My thinking brain is the servant of gut bacteria
    Who are constantly clamoring to obtain and engorge
    Sugars and starches in all their forms.
    They whisper sweet nothings in my ear
    "Wouldn't a freshly baked hunk of sourdough
    go well here. One slice won't hurt."
    On every fork along this road to the kitchen
    A sign asks me, "Do you want to feed the enemy?"

Week 25

Living Is Walking

> Clearly examine the blue mountains walking and examine your own walking. Examine backward walking and investigate the fact that walking forward goes on all the time.

As discussed, walking forward is projecting the mind outward. The mind is always pursuing something. In the morning, it is natural to project the mind forward. "Today, I'm going to do this or that." But when I think about the future like this, I'm thinking about a projected self.

It's the same with thinking about the past. If I'm still longing for something I experienced in the past, or if I'm criticizing myself for something I did, I'm still thinking about a projected self. Dogen says that thinking about that projected self is the mind taking a forward step. It is the mind leaving this moment in time and space. When we do this, we are not realizing our true self, the self that exists here and now.

Sometimes it sounds like Zen is saying walking forward is bad, that we should only walk backwards. But we can't walk backwards all the time. That is ridiculous. We'd fall down and hurt ourselves. We'd get lost and fail to meet important commitments. Dogen tells us to realize that walking forward and backward has always been going on, is going on right now and will continue to go on in the future.

So, we walk backwards *and* we walk forwards. We are given this brief life and the opportunity to do something with it. Walking backward and walking forward is what living is, what living has always been. Understanding this will make walking forward different and it will make the way you live your life different.

Most of us want to be of service, we want to express kindness and love and be of benefit to others. We don't want to be destructive, or participate in, or support destructive activities. When we know forward and backward walking, we see this whole reality that Dogen is talking about. We see the on-goingness of our lives. That's what love is. Love is birth and death. Love is appearing and disappearing. Love is caring for each other and knowing that we are one family in existence, that we are all the same, that each existence depends on every other existence.

So, everybody is constantly walking forward and backward. With Zen practice, we can really appreciate walking forward and backward. Practice changes our walk, and our motivation. With practice, thought, speech and action lose self-centredness and gain compassion. This way of being could have far reaching effects on so many of the problems that we face at this time in history.

Suggested Practice:
Living Is Walking

Take the backward step by beginning and ending each the day with sitting meditation and by allowing mindfulness practice to penetrate all activities in between.

· · · · · · · · ·

A week of surrender to the winds of change and clogged plumbing.
Both steps forward, out of the routine, creating opportunities for adjustment of schedules, attitudes, and time.
Kitchen sinks take on new meaning when you can't use them – the whole life of the house changes to accommodate.
The winds – the incredible winds of change – climate change, personal change as the winds and waters swirl taking me out of the garden to watch hail fall on the flowers.
Life in the moment adapting, adjusting, meditating on reactions.
There is no backward in a thunderstorm there is only now.

· · · · · · · · ·

Dogen's Koan #28

Monk: What is the essence of the Buddha Way?
Teacher: A dragon howling in a withered tree.
Stepping backwards
Self recedes into a withered tree
leaving behind dried leaf-skeletons
hanging from shrinking branches
leaving behind yes and no
leaving behind neither yes nor no,
leaving behind both yes and no
dropping all the maybes and what-ifs
curling deep into beyond the beyond
resting, relaxing, studying
withdrawing the sitting bones
a baby dragon gestating in the mud.

Week 26

Sitting With the Mystery

If walking had ever stopped, Buddha ancestors would not have appeared.

HERE, "BUDDHA ANCESTORS" MEANS the profound depth and reality of our human lives. He goes on.

> If walking had ended, Buddha dharma could not have reached the present day. Walking forward never ceases; walking backward never ceases. Walking forward doesn't obstruct walking backwards. Walking backwards doesn't obstruct walking forward. This is called the mountains' flow and the flowing mountains.

With walking backwards, we realize the eternal awesome presence of everything, of every life, of every moment. When this realization comes, we stagger backwards in awe. The universe is so immense, and we marvel that we are here at all. Just look at where we are! Why is all this here? Who could imagine such a universe? People blithely talk about evolution but what are they saying? They are saying that this immense universe happened through an unbelievable process that nobody can quite imagine, let alone figure out. Knowing this mystery in your bones is taking the backward step.

Taking the forward step is doing something in our lives. Backward stepping and forward stepping depend on each other.

When you realize this unity, nothing ever goes wrong. I don't mean that you don't get sick or die. It is still true that if you lose someone you love, your world comes to an end. But in the deepest sense, nothing ever goes wrong because you know that life and death are just the mountains walking. Loss happens as we go forward in living, but we can get through it because gain and loss are always going on. Everybody experiences them. So, we say, "I'm ok. It's hard, but I'm ok." We can do anything together because we know and accept that gain and loss are always going on.

Times now on our planet are difficult. But there is never a better time than a difficult time to meditate and develop Zen practice. It is in the hard times that the depth of understanding and realization that the benefits that practice delivers are fully realized. It's funny, because I've noticed that when people are having a hard time, they stop practicing. They tell me that they haven't been sitting because the stuff that is happening in their lives distracts them and takes them away. They say they don't have the time to do Zen practice.

I smile, and say, "I understand." And I do. But actually, it is the opposite. I, too, have been in terrible times when the only thing I could do was sit down and meditate. And meditation is what saved me, because during those tough times, here I am, stable in my practice, holding a bigger vision, knowing how to manifest love and caring. We are all born with a desire to be a loving person, but it takes effort in practice. That is what Dogen is saying.

Suggested Practice:
Sitting With the Mystery

When things get tough, sit down and meditate.

· · · · · · · · ·

This week, my awareness has narrowed down to opposing the publishing of biblically text-proofed hate literature against the LGBTQ+ community in our local newspaper. I've been taking the forward step by asking others to support my insistence that our local newspaper make a public statement about its hate speech policy, and refrain from publishing anything that encourages hatred towards any group. Such rhetoric is dangerous. Because of this, I completely identify with what Norman says about hard times. "It is in the hard times that the depth of understanding and realization that practice delivers are fully realized." After ranting and raving about the "religious lunatic" who sent this letter to the editor and about its harmfulness, not only to the people that he has targeted, but also to the love teachings of Christianity, I did a lot of zazen.

Meditating and reading this week's texts while dealing with such ugliness helped me to take the wider and more compassionate view. Ranting and raving didn't help – it just made me more agitated, but this gift of insight from my zazen leaves me with a settled feeling and has dissolved my rage and fear. How miraculous is that?

Week 27

Drop Conditioned Beliefs

> Green mountains thoroughly practice walking and eastern mountains thoroughly practice traveling on water.

HAVE YOU EVER NOTICED that animals can't live an unreal life? We humans can wake up one day and realize that we've been living an unreal life for the last thirty years. This often happens when people begin Zen practice, or when they hear the wisdom of Buddha's teachings. Dogen says that mountains thoroughly practice being exactly what they are. Part of our limitation is that we don't thoroughly practice; or, in other words, we don't thoroughly live our lives. But mountains do.

Anyone who has attended a full Zen retreat knows how wonderful it is to live a Zen life punctuated by the sound of a bell guiding our daily routine. It's like floating through time, and if you are steeped in Zen literature, phrases from the teachings may suddenly come to mind and brighten your view. Dogen started out this essay with the phrase, "mountains are mountains" in mind. So here he is thinking about another phrase, "Eastern mountains are walking on water."

We feel slightly off balance when Dogen talks like this. Our fixed idea is that mountains don't walk; mountains don't travel on water. That's absurd. But here he goes on as if mountains walking on water are just a matter of fact. If you really examine mountains, you'll see that his words are true. Mountains do travel on water. They travel on clouds; they travel on streams and they travel on snowmelt. Every leaf of every plant on every mountain is water. Water causes constant motion, constant decay and renewal. This is the mountains' thorough practice.

> Keeping its own form without changing body and mind, a mountain always practices.

This brings us back to the *feeling* of mountains, to the practice of sitting in zazen through everything that arises, in the same way that a mountain is steadfast thorough all weathers. As our sitting practice deepens, we sit steadfast through all conditions: happiness, sadness, joy, hope, despair, grief and doubt. We just sit still and discover that we have the power to do so through all conditions – like a mountain does. We endure as a mountain endures. Dogen says that's how mountains always practice everywhere.

But what about mountains travelling over water? Here Dogen asks us to deepen our understanding, to broaden our view.

> When your understanding is shallow you will doubt the phrase 'green mountains are always walking.' When your understanding is immature you are shocked by the words 'flowing mountains.' Without fully

understanding the words 'flowing mountains,' you drown in small views and narrow understandings.

Dogen invites us to let go of limiting beliefs and view our lives through a new and deeper lens.

Suggested Practice:
Drop Conditioned Beliefs

Reflect on how your conditioned beliefs limit freedom of thought. Imagine how your freedom would deepen if you dropped those beliefs, and simply observed the world as-it-is.

· · · · · · · ·

In my late twenties, I awakened to the futility of chemically altering my perception. I thought sobriety and a higher power were the final awakening. In my thirties, I awakened to the destructive power that my family of origin had on life. I thought psychotherapy and depth psychology were the final awakening. In my forties, I awakened to the gift of zazen and Zen practice. I thought sitting and living monastically were the final awakening. In my fifties, I awakened to teaching zazen and Zen practice. I thought realizing the bodhisattva life was the final awakening. In my sixties, I awakened to the unreality of all of that. I thought finding the eternal in the moment was the final awakening. In my seventies, I continue my practice of awakening.

Week 28

Our Lives Are Bigger Than Our Problems

WE ARE NOW more than halfway through this study of Dogen's *Mountains and Rivers Sutra*. We have seen how Dogen offers an expanded view of what it means to be alive and to engage practices that explore that expanded view. He says,

> You don't understand that mountains are like flowing water because you are drowning in small views and narrow understanding.

He is talking about us. He is saying that when we have that sinking feeling that we are drowning in the hardships of our lives, it is because we are hemmed in by the limited way in which we view our lives.

He goes on.

> Yet, no matter how we feel about our lives, mountains will always manifest their own life force.

In other words, even though we are stuck in our small views and limited understanding, the mountains are just fine. Unlike us, they aren't ranting and saying, "Hey wait a minute. That's not right. We are still flowing. What's the matter with you? You are not giving us credit." In this way, we humans insist that others see us the way we want them to see us. But mountains are not like that. They don't care how others see them. They just continue to manifest their form and life force.

Of course, this is also true of us. Even when we protest and complain, we too are manifesting our life force. No matter how much we complain about our health, the cost of food, or the inconsiderate actions of others, the miracle of living goes on. Awareness of this simple truth is the secret to how we can bear our own, and our friends', suffering. Even if we don't understand why we suffer, we can know that life goes on no matter what, doing what life needs to do. We can rest in the certainty that life is always life, and it goes forward without concern about how we want our own situation to be.

Dogen continues.

> There is walking, there is flowing and there is a moment when a mountain gives birth to a mountain child.

This is beautiful, but what is he talking about? He is reminding us that even though life continues to vacillate between joy and sorrow, every now and then something happens, and we have a moment of transformation, a moment, if you will, of enlightenment. Diligent effort in Zen practice will transform our lives, so that every now and then we will have a moment when we experience total awakening. Even though transformation is constant when we practice, even though life itself is change, sometimes a surprising birth occurs and "a mountain gives birth to a mountain child."

Suggested Practice:
Our Lives Are Bigger Than Our Problems

On those days when you feel overwhelmed by life's difficulties, let go of worrying about your problems and remember that when we are immersed in our own suffering, we have taken a narrow view with limited understanding. Our lives are bigger than our problems.

Week 29

Take the Bigger View

In *Mountains and Rivers Sutra*, Dogen tells us that there are hierarchies of understanding. If you are in the mountains you might see grass, trees, rocks and remote mountain cabins. Then you might realize that these are only separate things that make up mountains, and that there is no such thing as a mountain. "Mountain" is just a word. Dogen says that realizing there is no such thing as a mountain, that there are only trees, rocks, paths and creeks, doesn't take our understanding far enough.

Then he goes deeper,

> even if you view mountains as the seven-treasure's splendor, this is not returning to the source.

The next level you might understand is that grass, trees, rocks and remote mountain cabins are simply various combinations of the elements and atoms that make up our planet. Then, you see mountains a bit more deeply. But Dogen says that even that level of understanding is not "returning to the source."

Then, he goes beyond the physicality of mountains and tells us that even if we recognize the spiritual value of mountains and deeply know their sacredness, we have still not gone far enough. The truth about mountains is even deeper because these levels of understanding are nothing but conditioned views.

But these views are exactly what he has been talking about so far in his essay. So now he is saying that what he has been teaching us is just another conditioned view.

> These ways of seeing a mountain don't represent true understanding.
> They are merely looking through a bamboo pipe at a corner of the sky.

This is a typical Zen metaphor. There is the vast sky, the boundless sky, the beautiful sky where all kinds of things are happening. A cloud goes by. Birds soar. Breezes caress. There is no end to the sky. You can look at the sky forever. It turns pale blue in morning. It displays all the vibrant colours of sunsets and dawns. As humans, we are made in such a way that our hearts can be broken open by looking at the sky.

However, for some reason, we forget to see the whole sky. Instead we have a bamboo tube, two centimeters in diameter, and whichever way we look, we are always looking through this tube with the mistaken understanding that we are seeing our whole life. Dogen is telling us that even if we know that "mountain" is only a word, the objects on mountains are only elements and atoms, and that mountains are sacred, we still don't get it. All these views limit our understanding in the same way that looking through a bamboo pipe limits our view of the sky.

Suggested Practice:
Take the Bigger View

Take some time to really study the sky from a place where you see the horizons. After twenty minutes, look at the same sky through a straw and then reflect on what this says about the way you see your life.

·········

Like a baby discovering her toes
reaching out to touch what she sees
stopping a racket by covering her ears.
I can wiggle and grab! I can move!

Like a child learning to talk, read and write.
Combining and arranging sounds and symbols
clicking teeth and tongue to make words come out.
I can talk! I can think! I can create!

Like a teen-ager tempering desire
calming urges and hormones that push hard
against all warnings of rational thought.
A moment of wisdom. I can resist!

Like a middle-aged woman dissolved into work
her gaze getting fogged by the dust of the world
awakening her eyes to receive the bright sky.
A moment of vastness. I can choose!

Like a crone as still as a crane
Like wild rice calling to the mountain osprey
Like three otters swimming near the bulrushes
Like underwater milfoil growing in the night.
I can enter the mystery completely.

Week 30

Enlightenment Is Nothing Special

DOGEN LISTS SEVERAL WAYS of understanding the Zen teachings. He presents three traditional approaches to understanding. The first phrase he discusses in this paragraph is *turning circumstances and turning the mind*.

Zen teachers before Dogen said that what we need to do is "turn circumstances and turn the mind" and not allow circumstances of daily life and thoughts that appear in mind to turn us. But Dogen says no, that's not it; that's not what the Buddha taught. In his next sentence, he refers to a teaching that many Zen masters of his day emphasized, *seeing into mind and seeing into essence*.

These words are a translation of the Japanese word, *kensho* or enlightenment experience. *Buddhas grumble when you idealize enlightenment*, says Dogen. Only people who know nothing about Zen would promote kensho. Nothing could be more harmful than teaching the dharma by promising enlightenment.

Here, Dogen denies the common view of Zen practice that he encountered when he travelled to China to train with the Chinese masters. At that time in China, many Zen teachers emphasized the enlightenment experience. We still see this today in the pop spirituality movements that encourage us to imagine that we can attend a week-end workshop to have an enlightenment experience that will free us from suffering. Dogen says, *This is not the Buddha dharma*.

Finally, he says, *Confined words and phrases do not lead to liberation*.

Here he is referring to the popular Zen practice of studying koans, the teaching stories about the realizations of past Zen teachers. Dogen is denying that the powerful insights that come from koan study lead to liberation. With these words, he wipes away everything that previous Zen teachers have taught, and he has set us on the edge of our seats. If those three ways of practice don't free us, what does? Dogen answers that question.

> There is something free from all of these views. Green mountains are always walking and eastern mountains travel on water.

This is astonishing. He is telling us that the answer to the mystery is a poetic phrase. In effect, he is saying "When I say green mountains are always walking and eastern mountains travel on water, I am not talking about all this other stuff. I'm not using Zen phrases in the same way. You must study this in detail."

In other words, setting up a Zen phrase or enlightenment experiences as more important than an ordinary phrase or ordinary living is a mistake that leads to all kinds of goal-seeking, hierarchies and harmful dynamics. He doesn't deny that there is a transcendent and powerful life full of gratitude, but that life is no other than the one we are living in this very moment, right here.

Suggested Practice:
Enlightenment Is Nothing Special

In the next week notice the various ways in which you look to the future to bring you lasting happiness. Then see true happiness right here, right now.

·········

Happiness
The baby was due on the 25
No arrival
Inducement date was yesterday
Nope
It is supposed to be now – right this minute
I have no idea what is happening
I wait
I am happy every day – the parents are
healthy, we grandparents are friends
together we wait.

Week 31

We Are Mother to All Beings

NO MATTER WHAT YOUR LIFE IS LIKE, if you look at one day in detail you would see many riches. So much happens in one day. Even in a half hour of meditation, we encounter endless thoughts, memories, and visions of the future. James Joyce knew this. In his novel, *Ulysses*, he devotes 700 big tiny-print pages to one day in the life of his protagonist, Leopold Bloom. In *Mountains and Rivers Sutra*, Dogen advises us against limiting ourselves to a single way of seeing spiritual life. Spirituality, he tells us, is more than a specific religion. It is like *a stone woman giving birth to a child at night*.

If we take this phrase as a metaphor for spiritual awakening, it helps to notice that it happens in darkness, in the unconscious. It happens without our noticing it, in a way that we could not have anticipated. It happens in ordinary human experiences, such as giving birth to a child. Dogen asks,

> At the moment of giving birth to a child, is the mother separate from the child?

No, because at the moment of giving birth, two beings exist as one being. The mother's mind is overwhelmed and affected by the child's mind, and the child's mind is overwhelmed and affected by the mother's mind. As human beings, we are a family. It may seem that we are different, but if you looked at the earth from lightyears away, you'd think that all humans are the same. We all do the same things. We eat. We sleep. We walk upright. We are all exactly the same. So, isn't it weird that we fight and go to war, like humans do?

Dogen is suggesting that becoming a mother is a model for spiritual transformation. When a woman gives birth, she becomes a different person with different motivation. Mothers no longer think of themselves as being only themselves. Their identities now include the identity of their children. This is a psychological, physiological, spiritual fact that comes from the deep heart of our species. Without this, our species would not go on. In other species, mothers give birth and then move on. It works for them, but in humans it doesn't work. Unless mothers feel like mothers, we humans won't go on.

Dogen's proposal of motherhood as a model for spiritual development is radical. Usually, spiritual quest involves a hero who leaves his family, rejects all help, and then disappears into the sunset. But spiritual transformation isn't about having a fantastic experience that makes us smarter than others. It's about the common events of human life – such as giving birth. My heart is open, now. I identify with others, now. I have kindness and concern for all beings, now.

Dogen is saying that every time our practice goes deeper, it is because we are going deeper into feeling a profound motherly care for others.

Suggested Practice:
We Are Mother to All Beings

Imagine a world in which everyone saw all beings as their children or grandchildren. What then?

·········

One week ago, my son and his wife became parents
In watching them go through the birth, in holding the new soul, the truth of the teaching was alive,
it sat breathing in my arms, it was reflected in the eyes of everyone present.
The miracle of life happening every day, all around me (us) and the vibrant
life force that we all share is pulsing if I can be quiet and listen, feel, understand
that I, too, am the force, giving life to others around me, living the great passage called a lifetime.

·········

I care for seedlings, like they are tender fetuses and newborns
I nourish Mana squash plants, like they are babies developing brains
I protect tomatoes from imminent disaster, like they are toddlers on the run
I guide climbing beans like they are teens seeking the sun
I watch the corn stalks grow, like a sangha in the zendo

Week 32

Zen Is Logical

IN THE NEXT SECTION of *Mountains and Rivers Sutra*, Zen master Dogen takes to task other Zen teachers of his day who say that the old teaching stories of Zen cannot be understood logically, that the purpose of Zen stories is to defeat logic. Dogen uses the story of Nansen, an 8th Century Zen master, to make his point and he complains that too many Zen teachers teach the story as an example of how logic cannot help a student understand Zen. Too many teachers have the idea that Zen is illogical, that Zen is not a religion because it is beyond religion, or that Zen is beyond the scriptures that contain Buddha's words.

It's true that there are certain sayings in Zen that make it look like Zen stories are meant to destroy the logical mind and enable students to leap past logic to some other transcendent realm of realization – and beyond. Dogen says this is totally ridiculous, and many of his essays logically explain stories that other teachers say are not logical. But Zen Master Dogen doesn't explain things in the way we usually explain them. In a way, the traditional Zen phrases, such as *a stone woman giving birth to a child at night*, are so illogical that the only way to understand them is to reach an understanding that is beyond our ordinary and limited way of understanding. An example story follows.

> Nansen, a Chan (Zen) teacher who lived in 8th Century China, was working in the fields harvesting rice.
> A student interrupted him to ask, "What is the true way."
> Nansen held up his sickle and answered, "I got this sickle for thirty cents."
> The student replied, "That's not what I asked you. I asked, 'What is the true way?'"
> Nansen went back to working and said, "My sickle works very well."

This story goes directly to Dogen's insistence on logical explanation because the student insisted that Zen is beyond Nansen's words about his sickle. But Nansen says that truth is not some transcendent and other-worldly epiphany. Truth is right here. Truth is completely giving oneself to this work, right here, right now.

Nansen is saying, "I'm answering your question about the way, and the answer is in this sickle that I got for thirty cents. His answer includes everything: the world of commerce, the world of tool making, the minerals in the tool and, indeed, the whole reality of life, itself.

"It's all right here," he is saying. Don't make some transcendent illogical world that becomes its own kind of tyranny. Just find the truth that is right in front of you.

How beautiful and simple is that!

Suggested Practice:
Zen Is Logical

Several times in the next week pick an activity, such as washing dishes or cleaning the garden. Look deeply into it to discover how much of the world is present in that activity. Notice when you enter into an understanding that is beyond your normal way of seeing that activity.

Week 33

In Zen We Have No Truth

In Zen, we have no special truth, no transcendent understanding that only we have. All we have is our lives and our full engagement with them. That is the only truth we have, and it is the same truth that everybody else has. When we enter Zen practice, we enter our lives as deeply as we can, more deeply than we did before we found Zen, because practice heals our lives. In *Mountains and Rivers Sutra*, Dogen makes it clear that it's been that way since the beginning, and that the Zen ancestors lost their way when they started setting up a special Zen understanding of a special Zen truth.

Even now people make the same mistake. They set up a Zen master as someone who has a unique understanding. They imagine that a Zen teacher has realized something they haven't. But to think that way is to deny what the Buddha taught. When Buddha sat under that Bodhi tree and entered enlightenment, he realized that his life was only a miniscule point in time and space, and it is unspeakably wise, beautiful, and healing. There is nothing unique about it. And he taught that everyone has their own amazing miniscule point in time and space. Buddha wasn't thinking that his experience was special. When he taught, he was simply trying to describe what he had experienced.

When we first read Zen stories, koans, we think they are illogical, and that they transmit a special truth. But Dogen is always telling us that the Zen koans are not illogical. He agrees that they are hard to understand, but there is a way to understand them. Not in our usual way of understanding, but in another way that uses language differently. And this other way is truly transformative.

Dogen also says that we can never come to the end of understanding the Buddha's teachings. In Zen, there is no equivalent to the Apostle's Creed that dictates what we must believe to be true. Truth in Zen is beyond doctrine. It is beyond our ordinary way of understanding. But, says Dogen, if we throw away our ordinary capacity to understand, and abandon ordinary language, we misunderstand our lives. We misunderstand Buddha's teaching. Even though truth is beyond doctrine, Zen students spend a lot of time trying to understand Buddhist teachings. And the study is never over.

Like study, zazen, which is the heart of Zen practice, is never over. We don't do zazen once and then not do it again. We don't say, "I did that yesterday. Why should I do it today?" That would be absurd, because like the teachings, zazen is inexhaustible and endlessly illuminating. We go on with it even if we feel we've reached the end. Zen has no final destination, no final truth.

Suggested Practice:
In Zen We Have No Truth

Take some time to reflect on a spiritual principle that you believe you understand. See if you can look beyond your understanding of that principle and enter a brand-new world.

Week 34

Mindfulness Is a Spiritual Practice

Dogen identifies various religious views that he feels are a mistake. He writes that nihilism, the idea that life is meaningless, is a destructive wrong view. If we believe that nothing matters, that actions have no consequences, that when we're dead and gone it's over, there is no reason to develop moral behavior. It stops mattering whether or not our words and actions cause harm.

Another wrong view is pure naturalism, the belief that spiritual training and practice is not necessary because if you can be spontaneous, your wisdom will naturally come out. Dogen complains that there is too much of this Taoist view in the Zen teachings of his day. In Zen, he insists, there is a training path to help us cultivate awakening. I compare this view to becoming an accomplished pianist. First, you work hard practicing scales and chord formation and changes, next you study harmonic theory and perfect techniques, and then finally, after many years, when you have mastered all of that, you let go of the training. Your body and mind become a natural vehicle for the music. Dogen felt that the Zen teachers of his day were throwing away diligent training. He accused them of naturalism, a classical mistake in Buddhism.

In the thirteenth century, the Zen establishment lost imperial support, so it needed a new class of people to help finance the monasteries and temples. They formed an alignment with the intellectuals and literati who were into Taoist poetry and the Confucian classics. Many Zen teachers were reshaping Zen for those intellectuals, and they presented Zen as a very sophisticated literary game that had to do with knowledge of classical Chinese literature.

Dogen had no respect for that approach. He was completely committed to Zen as he had learned it from his teacher, Rujing, in China. He believed that meditation and practice, as he taught it, was the epitome of the Buddhist tradition, that Zen was not a new school but the original practice of Shakyamuni Buddha, and that the Japanese literati were making Buddhism into something it was not.

Nowadays, Zen is a marketing tool. It has become pop psychology and its spiritual value has diminished. The mindfulness movement insists that its ancient Buddhist practices are not based in religious consciousness. Teachers say, "Forget the Buddhist religion, just teach its psychological practices and meditation." They make the same mistake that Dogen wrote about.

Mindfulness and meditation that ignores Buddhism misses the power and depth of a ritual life that extends back 2600 years. Dogen saw that the intellectuals of his day were throwing out the deepest part of Zen practice to gain financial support. Similarly, the vigorous marketing of mindfulness practices has diminished meditation into a pop psychology improve-your-business fad. This robs a deeply spiritual religious teaching of its virtue and power.

Suggested Practice:
Mindfulness Is a Spiritual Practice

Whatever spiritual practice you undertake, consider deeply whether it is truly expressive of its spiritual roots, or has it been watered down for marketing purposes.

· · · · · · · · ·

My life is changing so fast; in the last few weeks I feel like I have let go of you. Not because of you, but because life has sped up to the point where I don't seem too focused on the moment – it is like trying to find time in the eye of the tornado.

I am sharing all of this because I don't think I can commit to the practice. This has been a very meaningful journey through time. I thank you all and it seems strange to think of goodbye but I don't really know what else to say.

· · · · · · · · ·

Our inner lives have been so intertwined through this process, and all we've done is read 700 words a week and shared reflections on those words. Over the last 34 weeks, this simple process has had, for me, profound impact on where my awareness lands from moment to moment.

So off you go into the world, never to be seen again in this Ethernet practice realm. The fact that we will not see you again, makes your leaving here a little bit like a death that restructures our world. Of course, I know I will see you again, but, in terms of this practice realm, it is as if you have died.

Your presence here has been meaningful, you and your words have mattered deeply and have had such inspirational consequences on my life. I do wish you would reconsider.

Week 35

Is Zen Buddhism?

WHEN HE RETURNED to Japan from China, Dogen criticized the monks he met, who insisted that Chan, the Chinese root of Zen, was over-rooted in Buddhism, that it was simply a new form of Taoism, and that its practices were just another method to realize the primary goal of awakening to spontaneous enlightenment. Dogen felt that setting up enlightenment as Zen's primary goal ignored the fact that Zen is an expression of Buddhist teaching. He believed that practice must include a deep study of Buddhist scriptures. He insisted that presenting Zen as nothing other than an aesthetic spiritual experience robbed people of the healing potential of Buddha's teaching.

Zen is *not* about the arts. The study of Zen writings is *not* a literary exploration. Nor is it a new age self-help system. To adopt that view is to eliminate significant aspects of Zen and realize only one dimension of the practice. Let's be clear: Zen is Buddhism and Buddhism is Zen.

Dogen saw himself as responsible for conveying Buddhism to Japan and was adamant that the Japanese people get it right. But we live in North America where the marketplace manipulates our values. If an object or an idea or a process sells, it's good. In the marketplace, Zen has been reduced to a marketing tool for no other reason than to link a product with something good. Here in North America, as in Dogen's 13th Century China and Japan, Buddhism has been dropped from Zen. But Buddhism is the thread that ties Zen to its origins. Consider a needle as it slips through fabric. If it holds no thread, what has it done to the cloth? Nothing. Buddhism is not irrelevant to Zen; it is the thread that holds the practice together.

In the long view of history, Zen Buddhism was introduced to the West less than fifteen minutes ago. It arrived with sincere intention to make the teachings understandable to the people who live here. North American teachers don't know a lot. We do our best to transmit Zen in a way that is understandable to the west, but that doesn't mean dropping the idea that Zen is an expression of the Buddhist teachings, nor does it mean divorcing Zen from its roots.

For these reasons, Zen centres all over North America and Europe follow practices that Dogen introduced to Japan in the 13th Century. We bow when entering the zendo, we burn incense, we sit and walk as the Buddha did, we chant in Japanese and we wear clothing designed for trainees in 5th Century India, in 8th Century China and in 13th Century Japan. We honour these ancient traditions and resist changing them because they take care of people who are looking for an authentic Zen practice.

Suggested Practice:
Is Zen Buddhism?

Try one traditional Zen practice in your daily life. The easiest is bowing. Choose one activity that you do regularly, like gardening or washing dishes, and bow before starting, and after finishing, the job. Investigate thoroughly the impact of this practice on your body/mind.

Week 36

Going Beyond Opposites

> Know that 'eastern mountains travel on water' expresses the bones and marrow of the Buddha ancestors. All waters appear at the foot of the eastern mountains. Accordingly, all mountains ride on clouds and walk in the sky. All mountains are the tops of the heads of all waters. Walking beyond and walking within are both done on water. All mountains walk with their toes on water and make them splash. Thus, in walking there are seven vertical paths and eight horizontal paths. This is practice realization.

THESE WORDS COME in the middle part of Dogen's *Mountains and Rivers Sutra*. This idea of mountains walking on water is a poetic statement of the dualism that is at the heart of all life: it is form and emptiness, yin and yang, enlightenment and delusion, hot and cold, good and evil. Usually we see these conditions and phenomena as being in opposition to each other. But here, in Dogen's essay, we have the mountains and waters traveling together.

If you truly look at mountains it is easy to see that Dogen speaks the truth. Snow melts from mountain tops so creeks flow down the mountains carrying small bit of the mountains in twists and turns that are both horizontal and vertical. When Dogen lived in China and when he settled in Japan, he lived in monasteries that were built high up the side of a mountain, so he was able to observe mountains closely. He saw that, in a sense, the mountains really are walking on streams, really are travelling on water. He saw that water collects into lakes at the foot of a mountain slope, and that the mountains sometimes ride above the clouds and walk in the sky. Many alpine hikers have had the experience of being on a mountain top looking down on the clouds.

Eiheiji, the monastery where Dogen lived and taught, sits high up the mountain overlooking the Japan Sea. Was he looking down on the clouds the first time he thought that mountains ride the clouds and walk the sky? They do.

In the last part of this quote, Dogen says all mountains walk with their toes on water and make them splash. Here Dogen is seeing and delighting in his realization that there is playfulness in mountains; that a spiritual quest can at times be like a child splashing toes in water.

For Dogen, Zen practice and realization, which is life, itself, doesn't divide reality into good and evil, right and wrong, black and white. Our lives are like mountains flying in the clouds. Our lives are mountains combining with water and walking beyond dualism, recognizing the oneness of all phenomena, and neither rejecting nor grasping any one aspect of it.

Suggested Practice:
Going Beyond Opposites

When you get stuck in one view of reality, consider how your view is connected to all other views.

· · · · · · · ·

I'm in Seattle *en route* to Paris. My view is full of dualistic thoughts. I am ashamed of my carbon footprint and thrilled with the idea of seeing all of my French family again. The "kids" are giving their mother a surprise birthday party, and I am part of the surprise.

How, as a sentient being, breathing the same air and watching the Earth's story, can I take this journey? The only answer I have is love. Marriages, deaths, births, binding us in love. I will make it up, pay my dues in service and nature. Right now, I am sticking my toes in the water and smiling to the heavens, dancing with the mountains and clouds.

· · · · · · · ·

"Our lives are like mountains flying in the sky."

This sentence evokes a deep feeling of liberation in my gut. It completely defies dualistic analysis and invites me to experience every moment in my life in a completely different way that is beyond pleasant or unpleasant, beyond good and evil, beyond opinions, beliefs and preferences, beyond the beyond. When I experience my moment-to-moment life in this way, no mental obstructions arise to fill my emptiness with wishes, regrets, analyses, agreements and/or disagreements with the teachings. Beyond praise and blame. Just this. Just this.

Week 37

We Can't Explain Our Lives

WE ALL HAVE our favourite stories, both from religious literature and secular literature. We can read a story, and somehow it changes our lives, so we never forget it. That story keeps coming back, and over the years we deepen our understanding and appreciation of it. This is how Zen literature works. Rather than explaining and analyzing, it is poetic, and like a good country song, it is meant to leave a short line or phrase that strikes you at a transformative moment in your life.

Zen stories, phrases and words are meant to be taken as something that we can attach our path to and be illuminated by. They can be a point of light in the middle of the darkness. In *Mountains and Rivers Sutra*, Zen Master Dogen is thinking of a story that illustrates the truth that there is no endpoint to Zen training. Practice and realization are one, so we don't have to feel discouraged because we haven't met a goal. Instead, we can take the light in from the beginning. The story that Dogen is thinking of is about Nanyue and Huineng, two Zen masters who lived in 7th Century China. Here's the story.

Nanyue comes to Huineng who asks, "What is it that thus appears before me?" In other words, "Who are you really?" Nanyue doesn't know what to say, so he meditates with this question for a long time. After eight years, he comes back to Huineng and says, "To explain would miss the mark." Huineng poses another question. "So, if it's like that, what is the point of practice and study?" Nanyue answers, "It's not that study and practice are pointless; it's only that they are unlimited" – like our lives.

We can't explain our lives; we can only live them. There is no end to the ways in which we try to define or grasp an understanding of this life. If we try to explain our lives, we just end up walling it up into an ingrained set of conditioned beliefs. Nor can we explain our spiritual practices because they too are endless. All we can do is exercise the gifts we've been given in this life. Our lives are wide open. They are like mountains playfully splashing their toes in the waters that flow down their sides and collect in lakes.

Suggested Practice:
We Can't Explain Our Lives

Reflect on a story or phrase that has helped you over a tough spot and into the next phase of your life.

· · · · · · · ·

A story that changed my life is *The Ship that Flew*. I read it when I was eleven or twelve. It's the story of a young boy who buys a pocket-sized ship and discovers that when he rubs it, it grows into a ship big enough to carry him and his friends anywhere they want to go. They travel through time and space and have adventures. This book gave me the idea that there is a world of the mind that is bigger than the one I lived in as a child. What a wonderful teaching that is. I am still exploring that world, and I remember sections of that book as if I had read it yesterday.

· · · · · · · ·

I am in France with the French family that "adopted" me 47 years ago when I was renting from their mother/grandmother. I have been here for eight days and tomorrow I go to Paris. I live here in my heart, as I live with those I love who have gone through all these years and changes; and although we have not been together in linear time, we have been together in heart. The young girl I met at age seven is now 53, and she and I spent the day at Saint Marie du Mer – the church of the black Madonna.

Week 38

Know Others as Others

> Water is neither strong nor weak, neither wet nor dry, neither moving nor still, neither cold nor hot, neither existent nor nonexistent, neither deluded nor enlightened.

DOGEN IS SAYING that water is beyond all opposition, description and explanation. Even modern-day science has been unable to completely explain water. Water, after all the talk and thinking about it, is just water. It's mysterious, really because water is one of the essential elements of life. It is in virtually everything – even rocks. And yet, what is it? We can't even say. We can't even settle on what shape or form it is.

> When water solidifies, it is harder than a diamond. Who can crack it?

When I first read this, I thought, 'Give me an ice cube. I'll crack it.' But maybe he means a glacier. It takes global warming to crack a glacier. So, in some ways what he is saying is true. Ice is so hard it can't be cracked.

> But when it melts, it is softer than milk. Who can destroy it?

Drop by drop water can wear away a rock face. Dogen asks us to consider the awesome presence of water and realize that it is not to be taken lightly. Water is the essence of all of life. It is not just another product to bottle and sell. When human beings really see water, they are thoroughly studying the moment; they are seeing the whole interconnectedness of life. Water couldn't exist without a place to exist in.

Likewise, each one of us has a place in the lives of all other beings. Each one of us is life itself. Dogen is reminding us that we all express aspects of each other. My understanding of another person is not who the other person actually is, and it is helpful in my relationships with others if I remember that. When I forget that, I make a mess of my relationships. If I let my partner and my friends just be my partner and my friends, I can know them for the unique people that they are. And if I am truly curious about them and how they experience the world, I can learn how they see themselves. I can be sure it is different from the way I see them. Not only that, but I can also be sure that they see water differently from how I see water. To understand that others' views truly differ from my own broadens my view of life. My world grows bigger; my life expands.

Suggested Practice:
Know Others as Others

The next time you drink a glass of water, take some time to reflect on the omnipresence of water and consider how precious it is. In that moment realize deeply that this water, in all its forms, sustains your own life and the lives of all that you love. Notice how gratitude for water can lighten the day.

·········

Yesterday I had a verbal go around with a man, a very intelligent man. It started when we all (four adults) tasted fresh pesto made with two types of basil – Italian and regular. I said the Italian was deeper, with a bit of smokiness. Another male adult said that "deeper" didn't get it for him – more like, earthier. Yes, yes, I said, that's it. Earthier. The other man tasted both and said – that one is better – and pointed at the Italian. I tried to encourage him to find words to express the experience, the smell and taste differences of the two. There was no way. He kept insisting that it was either good or not good. I finally realized that, maybe he was seeing the experience as a conceptual experience only, and I was conceptualizing it by seeing it as a sense-data experience. When I realized that, I stopped the conversation. We were so far apart in what we understood our conversation to be about that I saw no point in continuing. We parted friends.

·········

Paris: 1964
A small hotel, the air full of the intoxicating, seductive, smell of cafe au lait, warm croissants, streets that only speak to me in French, war-torn residue in the alleys, a museum that makes me cry, the perfect tart, walking into the sea and starting to float under a perfectly blue sky

Paris: 2019
 A world center of fashion and economy, beautiful women with deep, empty eyes, bums sleeping on doorsteps, immigrants in all sizes and shapes, tourists reading menus, looking for familiar foods, churches are locked, a gentle rain falls as I walk the cobble stones back to the hotel

Week 39

Loosen the Grip of Opinion

DOGEN TAKES SOME TIME to reflect on the different ways different beings see mountains and waters.

> Some beings see water as a jeweled ornament, but they do not regard jeweled ornaments as water.

He is being totally literal here. It really is true that some people can look at water and see it as a jeweled ornament.

So, is a sunlight ripple on a wave-tip a jeweled ornament, or is it water? It depends on who is looking. Another person might see the same ripples of light as wondrous blossoms; someone who is very ill might see it as a raging fire. A fish swimming deep along the lake bottom might see water as a palace or a pavilion that has no boundaries.

Dogen is reminding us that depending on causes and conditions – that is, on karma – we experience the world in our own way. We humans are so focused on ourselves that we don't realize that the world we see is not necessarily the world that exists; it is simply the world in concert with our own unique sensory apparatus and conditioned expectations. An ant crawling across the floor does not see a room full of people or imagine that our lives are more precious than the lives of ants.

So, the point of all this is that when we loosen our grip on our point of view, we can really understand that what we think is true is nothing more than a point of view. It is not a final description of the world. What we experience is simply the way the world appears in our lives right now. As we learn and change, our view of the world changes. If we truly realize this and refrain from insisting that our point of view is the only correct point of view, we can open to a whole new vision of the world.

Suggested Practice:
Loosen the Grip of Opinion

The next time you are completely immersed in a point of view, which you believe to be the absolute truth about any given situation, stop, open your mind, and consider another way of looking at the situation. Loosen your death-grip on your conditioned opinions.

Week 40

Our Lives Are Limitless

> Endeavours in the practice/realization of the way are not limited to one or two kinds. The thoroughly actualized realm has one thousand kinds and ten thousand ways.

HERE, DOGEN ADVOCATES for an awesome appreciation of an open view and tells us that there are an infinite number of ways to see our lives. Why would we choose one way; and especially, why would we want to choose a view that is uninspiring and difficult?

Many of us are convinced that this life is the only life possible, and choose a view that makes us unhappy. There is no good reason to do that. The truth is, there are a million ways to see our lives. It doesn't make sense to limit ourselves to one. Why not open to many ways of seeing, including the popular and unfortunate one that says we are inadequate, that our life lacks abundance. We might learn something about ourselves from that point of view, but it doesn't make sense to limit our view to that. It makes much more sense to give ourselves more space. The possibilities for understanding our lives are endless. Why not try them all out to see which one brings us a deeper, fuller life?

When we open ourselves to multiple possibilities, we begin to understand that there is no solid core at the centre. There is no essence or substance in any one view of our lives. There is just a constant arising and passing away of the different beings we encounter, and of the different views we adopt, and then there is release. When we realize this, we can also understand that in this one life that we share with each other, there is nothing that arises that is unrelated to everything else. Like water, our shared connections are everywhere. Our freedom depends upon each other.

In a similar way, our karma, that is our actions and their results, depends on others. But it doesn't end there. Dogen is saying that this is only one aspect of our lives. We are all tied up with family, community and culture, and that shapes our lives. But on the other hand, our lives depend entirely on our own bodies and minds. This is the paradox of Zen practice.

When I sit in meditation, I can intimately experience the details of my physical existence and the ongoing activities of my mind. But, at the same time my real life is beyond all those details. Everything that exists is, by definition, limited. When I sit zazen, I touch a life that is beyond all limitation. In meditation, I realize that the limited realm of my body and mind is a unique expression of that limitless reality. Knowing this, I can embrace my limitations, make intelligent use of them and not feel oppressed by them.

Suggested Practice:
Our Lives Are Limitless

Take some time to consider how you limit your possibilities by viewing your life in one way only.

· · · · · · · · ·

I spent last evening with a friend who has a seemingly intractable foot injury, and I noticed her aligning herself with the view that she is inadequate, and that her inability to generate financial abundance at this time is evidence of that. I paid attention as she worked this view into various self-identification statements that diminished her self-esteem. My friend has been such a bright light and it makes me sad to see her gravitating towards this self-critical and self-defeating view. It also annoys me that our culture has put financial wealth as the primary definition of abundance. From where I am looking, she has much abundance in her life that is beyond the financial – love and safety being the main things. I wish for her to give herself more space and open up to other possibilities for understanding her life during this difficult passage.

· · · · · · · · ·

Greetings from Italy – If you want to change your view, your possibilities, come, stay here for a while. Everything from how to drive, the possibilities of pizza, whether dogs are allowed in restaurants (and served a bowl of water), where volume and expression in spoken language takes on a whole new meaning (even if you can't understand the words – the language is alive), where the village church is always open and the bells ring through the night, where death notices are posted like old flyers on walls inviting you to come and say prayers.

Ten days ago I was in France – I could write about changing your mind, opening possibilities there, too, but now I am here. I am here in Damanhur, a spiritual eco-village that believes all humans are divine beings who come in with a purpose, a mission to both share and learn and evolve humanity's consciousness by connecting to their inner purpose and the living world of Gaia.

Week 41

The Teachings Are Everywhere

> When most human beings see water, they only see that it flows unceasingly. This is a limited human view; there are actually many kinds of flowing. Water flows on the earth, in the sky, upward and downward. It flows around a single curve or into many bottomless abysses.

HERE DOGEN IS POINTING to the enormous varieties of forms that water can take. Not only can we each see water differently, but water itself takes a million forms and engages in a million activities. It flows up and down, around curves, over waterfalls, into long wide rivers. It becomes clouds and when it falls to the ground it merges with lakes and rivers. Here Dogen is evoking a passage from a traditional Buddhist text called *The Lotus Sutra* in which Buddha teaches that the dharma, the compassionate teachings, are like rain that falls from the sky. Rain doesn't discriminate – it equally nourishes weeds and the food we grow. Everybody and everything is nurtured by the dharma rain, not just the people who are practicing Zen or any other religious path. The dharma is universally given, and in that way it is like water.

> The path of water is not noticed by water but is actualized by water. It is not unnoticed by water but is actualized by water.

Water manifests as water whether water knows it or not. The point is not whether water knows it is water, but that water always manifests as life. The same is true with us. The point is not what we are learning about our spiritual lives – it's not that important to know that stuff. What is important is that we fully live and embrace our spiritual selves.

To say there are places where water does not reach is the mistaken teaching of the people who think their religious path is the only true path. Water exists everywhere, even inside fire. Water also exists inside the mind, says Dogen, expanding his contemplation into the realization that water is not only a physical substance but is the spiritual principle that ignites the transformational moment that reveals the luminous truth shining in everything that exists.

When water falls to the ground it collects in gardens, rivers, and lakes. Only then does water become useful. Likewise, compassionate teachings collect, in books, in dharma centres and in realized teachers. When they collect in this way, we can make use of them in our spiritual lives. That's what a Zen centre is – a place where the teachings have been cultivated and nurtured through practice, and then pooled in a teacher.

Suggested Practice:
The Teachings Are Everywhere

Identify the places in your community where the waters of spiritual teachings have pooled and visit those places to taste their nectar.

· · · · · · · · ·

The other day on my walk, I had the sense that the entire Creston Valley is my monastery, a place where generosity, patience, spiritual discipline with body, speech and mind, and joyful effort for the happiness of others is nothing special – it's just my life – a life based in meditation and awake awareness. With this realization getting stronger, I'm finding a deep softening in my view of others, a wider opening of my heart to embrace the suffering of others, and an easy determination to offer my life to doing that. Happiness suffuses my whole being. The waters of spiritual teaching flow everywhere. The pools of spiritual teaching are everywhere – both in my body and in the body of the Creston Valley. We are all just one big body, and to take care of what is in front of me is no different than my right hand agreeing to pull my left hand out of the fire.

Week 42

Be Like Water

Ordinary people nowadays think that water is always in rivers and oceans, but this is not so. There are rivers and oceans within water. Thus, even where there is not a river there is water. It is just that when water falls to the ground it manifests the characteristics of rivers and oceans. So, don't think that only dharma centres and sages have water; it is everywhere. Also, don't think that where waters do not form rivers and oceans there is no dharma.

Here Dogen is saying that the teachings of wisdom are everywhere – not only in dharma teachings and in Zen temples. Wisdom is not concerned with past, present or future. It is not in any one specific place or religion. Truth appears spontaneously and springs up from moments that are grounded in deep integrity of thinking, speaking and acting. That's what truth is according to Dogen, and it is the only truth we need. This means that total flexible wisdom is available everywhere, all the time. It doesn't get stuck on anything: not on philosophy, religious writings, or on inspired religious leaders and teachers.

Dogen then points out that even though we think water only runs downward, it actually runs in all directions. It runs east, west, north and south and into all the points in between. It even runs up when it evaporates and rises to form clouds. This movement in all directions is constantly changing as we move through space. If we go to Japan, west becomes east and if we are on the Atlantic coast of France, the eastern coast of North America becomes west. Somehow all these fixed points on earth are not really fixed at all. They are constantly shifting and changing – like reality.

Heaven is not up there, and hell is not down there. Depending on the lives we live, hell or heaven is everywhere and can exist any time. They can also transform into each other at any time, depending on our state of mind. We don't need to get stuck with one way of seeing reality or with one set of beliefs. Zen is about letting go of self-limiting beliefs and self-definitions. It's about realizing that everything is always changing, always in motion and because of that, a truth that we can live by arises, like water, out of every person, place, thing and event that we encounter. The whole truth is with us right now. All we have to do is drop our conditioned way of seeing reality and pay attention.

Suggested Practice:
Be Like Water

Take some time to identify your core beliefs, preferences and opinions; and then reflect on how your life would be different if you dropped all that and allowed more flexibility into the way you view and live your life. Be like water.

·········

I am water.
Today I am rain, falling to earth, wanting to be absorbed, stabilized, balanced.
Last week at this time I was an evening mist in the alps, swirling around my illusions and dreams.
Winter is coming. Soon I will be a snowflake or the frozen edge of the lake.
I am all these manifestations because I have shifted time zones, said goodbye to many things and
opened the floodgates of possibility. I am swirling in the dark currents,
accepting that I am water. I am change, I am flowing but I want to find the shoreline and rest.

Week 43

Expand Your Limited View

> When dragons and fish see water as a palace, it may be like human beings seeing a palace. They may not think it flows. If an outsider tells them, 'What you see as a palace is running water,' the dragons and fish may be astonished, just as we are when we hear the words, 'Mountains flow.' Nevertheless, there may be some dragons and fish who understand that that the railings and pillars of palaces and pavilions are flowing water.

IN NORTH AMERICA, we don't have many palaces. Japan has many. Dogen is saying that when fish and dragons are in the water, to them, it might seem they have entered one of these ancient Japanese castles. Because fishes and dragons have only experienced water, it would make sense to them to conclude that the castle was just another manifestation of flowing water. If someone told them, "this isn't water, this is a castle," they might be as amazed as we are when Dogen tells us that mountains walk on water.

Dogen goes on.

> If you do not penetrate your superficial views, you will not be free from the body and mind of an ordinary person. You will not thoroughly experience the land of the Buddha ancestors, or even the land or the palace of ordinary people.

At first reading, these words sound harsh. But he means that the only way to go beyond the sufferings of body and mind such as confusion, aggression, hatred, anger, and fear that we won't get enough, is to go beyond our self-centred views. The Buddha taught that to be free of suffering we have to go beyond the conceptual frameworks and fixed beliefs that we have ingested and digested from our conditioning. It is these limited views that lead us to suffering.

There's a paradox here. Dogen is saying that being a Buddha is nothing more or less than being a normal human being who has transcended self-centred views. Unless we go beyond those views, we can't fully live the life of an awakened being. Unless we transcend our self-centred perspective, look out from our little worlds and let go of our small views about our lives, we won't know what it means to be fully in this world, living and dying, loving and hating, laughing and crying. The paradox here is that practicing the Buddha way and living an ordinary human life are one and the same.

Suggested Practice:
Expand Your Limited View

Notice when your world has shrunk into consideration of how you can get what you want when you want it, and when you do notice, raise your head and see the valley and mountains beyond. This looking outwards may broaden your view enough to help you transcend the constricting feeling of not having enough of what you need and want.

• • • • • • • • •

These days I'm a little muddled – today it's from a resurgence of full body arthritic pain – up until today, I had no excuse. I feel like my personality is deconstructing and all views are constantly shrinking and expanding from atomic particles to the macrocosmic universe. I'm just riding with it and not allowing fear to interfere in this undulating process.

Week 44

Let Go of the Self-Centred View

At this time, human beings deeply know that what is in the ocean and the river is water, but do not know what dragons and fish see and use as water. Do not foolishly suppose that what we see as water is used as water by all other beings. You who study the Buddha way should not be limited to human views when you see water.

HERE, DOGEN ISN'T JUST TALKING about water. He is talking about everything. He is pointing at the wonder of our human life. We are walking around on this tiny planet that circles a star in a galaxy that is just a tiny spot in an expanding universe that is so big we can't measure it.

Every school child knows this, but somehow, it is meaningless because we don't feel it from day to day. We don't enter into the awesome realization that in this endless space there are only six or seven billion of us, and if we want well-being, peace, safety and happiness, we have to get along with each other. Every one of us is made of the same chemical elements as every human, animal, plant and rock. We know this, but we don't know it. We forget how vast and how mysterious our flash-of-lightning moment is on this earth. From our limited self-centred view we imagine that we have to fight and kill each other for power, resources or to enforce a particular political or religious view. And we do this even though all we have is each other.

We know that every human being, in the process of conception and gestation goes through the same stages that every species goes through. So, we are amoeba and polar bears. We are eagles and pine trees. But our self-centred way of living has devastated this earth that provides food, air and water. We are probably the only species that knows this truth, so we have a unique role, both in addressing this world built on greed, hate and delusion and in creating a world built on generosity, kindness and wisdom.

Dogen tells us that when we get stuck in the view that we are the centre of the universe, and that nature is here to serve us, we get caught up in our self-centred view and lose our unique capacity to realize, appreciate, live out and find joy in the reality of our oneness with all of existence. He is telling us that we need to study water from a point of view that is larger than how it serves us humans. To understand Dogen, we have to go deeper than his words.

Suggested Practice:
Let Go of the Self-Centred View

When a situation in the world grabs your attention or a conflict arises in your life, examine how the situation or personal conflict has arisen from the habits of a self-centred view.

· · · · · · · · ·

Every conflict in my life has arisen from my self-centered view. As long as I see myself separate, I will react and defend myself, my ideas, my perception of space and my right to be apart from others. Having grown up in a world that sanctified separate identities how else could I be?

My great learning has been to understand that I am connected to everyone and everything, and the only real power I have is choice. My choices matter. I can help direct change in a direction that I understand to be better or of higher value, or not. I alone will not solve the perceived problem but my reaction, my choice, may help redirect the outcome.

I understand this relationship only in relation to my own consciousness; ERGO that is why doing this work is so important. I want to make better, more inclusive choices in life – for myself and for the world I flow through. Every day, every moment presents another moment of choice.

· · · · · · · · ·

Eight weeks to go and we will have realized completion of our shared year-long practice. I'm not just talking about exchanging emails; we have been connected in a way that is much deeper than that. And, in having found that connection, we will never lose it. I'm so grateful for our disciplined diligence, our flowing with the practice through its peaks and valleys. The seeds that our words have planted will sprout and grow individually in their own way in each of us. But the connection we have found will not change as we turn to our next year of practice. I'm remembering Pema Chodren's teachings on "Good in the beginning, good in the middle and good in the end." I'm noticing in me a lapse of virya, vigourous effort, as we enter the end, and in the noticing, resolving to exert an energetic wholehearted effort to make this practice as good in the end as it has been in the middle and the beginning. I hope you will join me.

Week 45

Spiritual Practice Awakens Space

DOGEN HAS BEEN WRITING about seeing mountains and rivers in a way that deepens our lives and expands our vision. In the last section of *Mountains and Rivers Sutra*, he writes about sages, people who live an awakened life, and introduces a new idea about how sages practice in the mountains and on water.

> Mountains have been the abode of great sages from the limitless past to the limitless present.

Before we can enter into an understanding of what Dogen is saying in this sentence, we have to appreciate what the word, "sages," means in Asian cultures. In China and Japan, a sage is like a mountain that has sat still and met everything that comes and goes with skillful means, that is free of all judgment. Dogen is also talking about the lineage of teachers who preceded him.

In Asia, there has long been a tradition of sages living alone and in groups in the mountains. After completing a certain level of monastic training, monks went into the mountains to deepen practice and to further develop wisdom. There were Taoist sages and Chan sages who were hermits, but many were not. They lived in large monastic establishments where you could visit and practice with them. When a three-month monastic training period was over, monks often burst out of monastic cloister to roam mountain trails, looking for famous Chan sages to debate the teachings. The sages were easy to find since they often adopted the names of the mountains where they lived. Thus, the sage became the voice of the mountain and the mountain became the essence of the sage. In other words, the sage awakened the mountain, and the mountain awakened the sage.

It's very much like coming to a Zen Centre or Zen temple in North America. When guests arrive, they not only see the zendo, but they feel the energy of past practice. Often when visitors enter the zendo for the first time, they comment on how peaceful it is because they are experiencing the accumulated effects of the mediation that has already taken place. Because of this, the zendo, like a mountain, is just as responsible for their awakening as the meditation practice that has awakened the building.

> Wise people and sages all have mountains as their inner chamber, as their body and mind. Because of wise people and sages, mountains are actualized.

Suggested Practice:
Spiritual Practice Awakens Space

Visit a place where people focus on spiritual practice. Notice the spiritual energy that others have left there for you. Allow that energy to deepen your practice.

· · · · · · · ·

The Temples of Humankind in Italy were carved out of the mountain, in secret for 16 years. They are a stunning catalog of all the ways humanity has searched for spiritual guidance and support. They are now open to the public.

I'm just back from Italy and continue to hold the energy and vision of Damanhur, where the temples are located along with an entire community dedicated to holding space for humanity, for the earth, for all sentient beings and for the deities that symbolize the quest of the human heart for answers and connections within the universe.

I am privileged to share in the energy and the future vision they hold in these times of radical, global change.

· · · · · · · ·

Sometimes, when I do my morning walk, I feel like the entire Creston Valley is awakened space, and in its "awakeness" awakens me – to the moment, to an expansion of bodhisattva intention in my chest, to receptivity, to being awakened by a rumpled man leading a sick puppy on a rope lead. At other times, when I'm confused, contracted and shaky, the zendo feels like a special place of deep refuge from the sufferings of the world. Its meditation-infused wood, its high ceilings and its zendo-mudra arrangement of cushions and candles and iconography awakens me. The emptiness of my robe awakens me. The space that my zafu takes up, no matter where I place it, is awakened, and awakens me from this ongoing dream of self-centredness.

We have been chanting the *Diamond Sutra* in the zendo. There's a verse in the *Diamond Sutra* that tells us that any place where the sutra is chanted is transformed into a stupa, a place that holds the relics of the Buddha. So each of us who is studying buddha, dharma, sangha is a living relic of the Buddha. How wonderful!

Week 46

Small Self Disappears

IN SOTO ZEN TEMPLES, each time we install a statue on the altar for the first time we do a ceremony called 'opening the eye.' The purpose of the ceremony is to symbolically awaken the statue so that when people enter the zendo they can really see the most enlightened qualities the statue expresses. At many lay practice Zen centers, the altar holds a statue of Kanzeon, the bodhisattva of compassion, not a god or a goddess, but a reminder of our own desire and ability to bring compassion into daily life. Often visitors enter a Zen Centre for the first time and report awareness of stillness and loving energy. Years of Zen practice has awakened the space.

Dogen says that a similar awakening of space happens to a mountain when a sage enters it. The mountain comes alive and the sacred nature of that mountain, that is naturally present in all mountains, awakens with the arrival of that sage.

> You may think that in mountains many wise people and great sages are assembled. But after entering the mountains, not a single person meets another. There is just the vital activity of the mountains.

Dogen is saying that the sages have become the mountains, and for this reason there is *no trace of anyone having entered the mountains.*

We all know the experience of small self disappearing into a beautiful setting or into an engaging activity that can be as simple as tending a tomato patch. It is a wonderful thing to disappear into a display of tulips while weeding a flower bed. Suddenly we are no longer separate from where we are or from what we are doing. When this disappearing happens, we no longer carry the burden of self. We are free of thoughts about what happened to us, who we are and what we want.

It really is a great burden to drag all the stuff of the past around. It's tiring to be defending ourselves or justifying our opinions and actions all the time. Family, community and country are always asking us to decide who we are, what we stand for and what we want. It can seem so important to have others recognize us and pay attention to us.

Dogen is telling us to "just say no" to all that. He's inviting us to drop our thoughts and disappear into our circumstances, into family, into community. He is giving us permission to be the spirit of the mountains and river valleys where we live. If we can do that, we will know the most profound rest that we have ever known.

Suggested Practice:
Small Self Disappears

The next time you are doing something that you love, notice how easy it is to disappear into the details of that activity. If thoughts about the activity or about another aspect of your life intrudes, just notice that and come back to full attention to what you are doing. Accept Dogen's invitation to let go of small self.

・・・・・・・・

The zendo gets busier and busier.
More views are opening to mountain mind.
Worlds transcend conventional time.

Before entering the zendo they stand at the gate
drop constructed lives on the deck
bow to the altar, bow to their zafu
bow to all beings, in all worlds, in all times.

Then entering the river, they sit facing the wall
Self-centred views begin to fall
thoughts slow down, until myriad worlds,
dissolve into silence as space unfurls and
disappears into time with no beginning, no end.
Only breath remains, alive and present.

Week 47

Mountains Don't Always Flow

When you see mountains from the ordinary world, and you meet mountains while in mountains, the mountains' head and eye are viewed quite differently. Your idea and view of mountains not flowing is not the same as the view of dragons and fish. Human and heavenly beings have attained a position concerning their own worlds that other beings may doubt or may not have the capacity to doubt.

DOGEN IS DRAWING OUR ATTENTION to the immense number of differences between all kinds of creatures and all the fixed and conditioned views that humans might have about any event or situation. He advocates not holding on to any views, but to respond according to the conditions that we meet at any given moment. In Zen, we call this "maintaining a flexible mind."

Do not remain bewildered and skeptical when you hear the words 'mountains flow,' but study these words with the Buddha ancestors. When you take up one view, you see mountains flowing; when you take up another view, mountains are not flowing. One time mountains are flowing; another they are not flowing. If you don't understand this, you do not understand the true dharma wheel of the Tathagata.

Dogen has been strongly advancing the idea that mountains flow. He has been really intense about pushing the point about mountains flowing because we don't usually think mountains flow. He has to make us understand this point through repetition and multiple examples. But by this time in the essay, we might well say, "Ok. I get it. Mountains flow. Forget about mountains flowing, already. I got it. In Zen, mountains flow."

But then he tells us not to get stuck on the idea that mountains flow. It is true that they do, but getting stuck on that truth locks us into a narrow view, because sometimes mountains don't flow.

Dogen is talking about duality and non-duality. He is reminding us that we can get stuck on non-duality, on the oneness of it all, and miss what is happening in the relationships right in front of us. We can fail to fully realize the situation we are in and harm ourselves and others. Then, because we no longer experience "the oneness," we can think we have failed in our practice.

But, sometimes mountains flow and we are compassionate and helpful. And sometimes the flow stops and we choose to leave a difficult relationship because, in that situation, it is the right thing to do. In leaving, we are not demonizing the other person or throwing our practice away. No, it is simply that we have realized that sometimes mountains flow in harmony; and sometimes they don't, so we take care of ourselves by leaving a situation without pressure and without hatred.

Suggested Practice:
Mountains Don't Always Flow

Study your circle of friends and acquaintances. Are you hanging on to any relationships that are no longer flowing harmoniously? If so, what then?

· · · · · · · ·

I am in Mexico attending my niece's wedding. Folks have come into Sayulita from all over the US, and in this gathering are many people I have known for a lifetime. Given this exercise, I see how much the relationships have ebbed and flowed over the years and, of course, none are the same as when they began. But the thing is, we are still together.

Many people are missing due to death, illnesses, and a few, including my estranged sister, by choice or circumstances. Those who are left in the game are here, truly present, to the new chapter that is unfolding before our eyes.

I watch the chapter begin and I wonder how many pages of this story I will share. Forty years of age difference is nothing to a mountain, but gives me a deep realization of the precious moments this life has given me, and I am so happy to be here sharing the moment. Bowing

· · · · · · · ·

Daido Loori in a dharma talk tells of a disciple who asked a Zen master, "Please teacher, tell me, why am I still suffering; I've done practice for years, I've studied all the important teachings, I'm doing my best to be good to others, but I still suffer. Please, tell me why?" The Zen master studied the situation deeply, then answered, "It's because you don't know the stench of your own shit." That was me; but no longer. Now, when shit is forming in my mind, that is, when I notice a shitty dysfunctional self-centred thought, I smell it right away and flush it down with awareness of the core delusions from which it arose.

Week 48

The Integrity of Trees and Rocks

ONE SECRET to understanding baffling Zen dialogues is to fully enter the dialogue and experience how the sage awakens the disciple from rigid adherence to a fixed view, or vice versa, how the student awakens the sage. If students insist that mountains are flowing, the teacher whacks them and says, 'No. Mountains are not flowing.'

At first, this seem paradoxical, but it is not, because one minute mountains are flowing and the next minute they are not. Maybe it isn't confusing when you know both sides so well that you realize that to say mountains are flowing is no different than saying mountains are not flowing. This is a really important point. Beyond duality we meet all conditions with flexibility, no longer thinking our view is the only true view. This is the virtue of practice experience. All that time practicing has been training our minds to realize that this life is a beautiful prospect, endlessly developing, endlessly ripening.

In Western culture, everything's good until we start to go downhill, get old, decrepit, lose intelligence, lose creativity. Our bodies fall apart, we start drooling, and everyone is embarrassed when they see us. In western culture, a human being peaks at age thirty-six or thirty-seven and then, at least physically, starts going downhill. But then you still live for another forty or fifty years. It's not a good design.

Zen training is not like that. If we look at a lifespan from a self-centred point of view, we reach our peak in our mid-thirties, and then everything after that is downhill. But if we look at that lifespan from the point of view of Zen training, it is a good design, because wisdom and compassion increase all the way up to the end, through the ending, and perhaps, beyond.

Dogen exhorts us to practice.

> An ancient Buddha said, 'If you do not wish to incur the cause for Unceasing Hell, do not slander the true dharma wheel of the Tathagata.' Carve these words on your skin, flesh, bones and marrow; on your body, mind and environs; on emptiness and on form.

This sounds like sound like Zen fundamentalism. If you slander, you will go into endless hell, so carve these words on your skin, flesh bones and marrow; carve them on your body, your mind, carve them on your surroundings; carve them on emptiness carve them on form. But then he says, in such a lovely way, that they are already carved on trees and rocks, on fields and villages. For Dogen, to slander the Buddha dharma, is to not live your life like a tree lives its life, or the way a rock lives its life – with full presence, with integrity.

Suggested Practice:
The Integrity of Trees and Rocks

Consider an argument or debate that you are involved in with family or in your community. Are you stuck on one point of view? Can you temporarily set aside your point of view to fully investigate the points of views of others?

· · · · · · · · ·

the secret

our secret is out in the open
it's everywhere for all to see
not hiding behind a story
not buried by traces of me

our secret flies high in the sky
sun, moon, clouds, wind, rain
offer night, liquid, and light
give blackbird song refrain

our secret is beneath our feet
where electrical impulse abounds
beans, potatoes and sweet peas
rise yearly out of the ground

our secret is out in the open
out there for all to see
not hiding behind a story
but caring for you and me.

· · · · · · · · ·

Older
Wiser
Don't argue
Listen
Many directions
Listen
New ideas
Many outcomes
Peace

Week 49

The Spiritual Power of Mountains

> Although mountains belong to the nation, mountains belong to people who love them.

WEALTHY PEOPLE MIGHT THINK they own their homes, but it is laughable, because they are going to be gone in a few decades, and the home will still be there. So, actually, the home owns them; and if you go to their home, if you are really there while you are there, their home belongs to you just as the mountains belong to those who love them. When you go anywhere and love where you are as your whole world, you own that place, and that place owns you.

> When mountains love their master, such a virtuous sage or wise person enters the mountains. Since mountains belong to the sages and wise people living there, trees and rocks become abundant and birds and animals are inspired. This is so because the sages and wise people extend their virtue.

That sage or wise person causes the mountains to come alive. This is so because sages and wise people extend their virtue. Virtue is an old-fashioned word that actually means power, the power of integrity. In ancient cultures, there was an understanding that rightness with the world and rightness with one's own life, created energy, and that this energy could be conferred. So, the power of the sages is conferred on the mountain and vice versa. Rulers have paid homage to sages and wise people to ask for advice and instructions. Disregarding the protocols of the usual world they ask a mountain sage to be their teacher.

It's like the tea houses in Japan. When you enter a teahouse, it has a tiny little entrance, so your sword won't fit in and you have to take off armor, sword and all the insignia of your military status. The teahouse, like the mountains, is a place where social standing doesn't matter anymore. When a ruler enters a tea house, he pays homage to the tea master; when a ruler enters the mountains, she pays homage to sages and mountains. Both tea house and mountains are apart from the human world and even an imperial ruler has no power over mountains or sage.

> At the time the yellow emperor visited Mt Kongdong to pay homage to Guangcheng, he walked on his knees, touched his forehead to the ground, and asked for instruction.

Even the Yellow Emperor wouldn't go to the mountains without bowing to his teacher in respect.

Know that mountains are not the realm of human beings or the realm of heavenly beings. Do not view mountains from the standard of human thought. If you do not judge mountains' flowing by the human understanding of flowing, you will not doubt mountains' flowing and not flowing.

With our current obsession with economics, the spiritual aspect of the environmental movement, which used to be so strong, seems to be growing weaker. It used to be that we really had a sense that our souls would be crushed if we don't preserve nature, so it wasn't even about the survival of the planet like it is now. It was that these mountains, these mountain streams, must be preserved for our spiritual need. We depend on them.

Suggested Practice:
The Spiritual Power of Mountains

At least once this week, make your way to a quiet place in nature, mountains, rivers, valleys, lakes or seaside, do sitting or walking meditation remaining mindful of the spiritual nurture that comes from nature.

·········

"mountains belong to the people who love them"

Wow! That is so beautiful and so true. I wish everyone knew this, because most of us naturally take care of what we love and what "belongs" to us. (Odd concept.) Or rather, if we really want to enter the deepest of teachings, not what belongs to us but, what is us. I am the mountains, the rivers, the valleys, the cities, the streets and those who live on the streets.

·········

The snow returned; it is now disappearing in the rain.

The local squirrels don't care. They continue their work of burying nuts. As I pass, they admonish me for my lazy ways. They're right, I hustle into the warmth of the house and make a pot of tea. I sit by the window and watch them work.

Week 50

Catching

> On the other hand, from ancient times wise people and sages have often lived on water. When they live on the water, they catch fish, they catch human beings, and catch the way. These are all ancient ways of being on water, following wind and streams. Furthermore, there is catching the self, catching catching, being caught by catching, and being caught by the way.

MUCH HAS BEEN DISCUSSED about Dogen's use of expressions like this. In his writing, Dogen, will occasionally remind us that words have virtue, and words are limited. He will take a word, "catch," and wring it through all of its possibilities, some of which seem absurd. It is like he is saying, 'Now that I am talking, I will remind myself, and you, that I'm talking in words; and you are understanding in words. Now I'll take the words all the way to the limit of words to remind us. Catching self, catching catching, being caught by the word catching and forgetting that catching is a word.

The word "catching" helps me understand what water is. Water is where you catch something, but in the water, you catch something so I've caught that concept. Now I am caught by it. When I know I'm caught by it, I catch the way. Now I'm going along here catching myself being caught, and now I'm free.

> Priest Decheng abruptly left Mount Yao and lived on the river. There he produced a successor, the wise sage of the Huating River. Is this not catching a fish, catching a person, catching water or catching the self?

It a beautiful thing that Dogen suggests here. When there is intimate accord in the relationship of disciple and teacher, it is like a sage entering the mountain. When a sage enters the mountain, the mountain loves the sage, and the sage loves the mountain. The mountain wakes up and the sage disappears. This is like the relationship between disciple and teacher. In it, we wake each other up. When both realize this mutual awakening, there is a degree of trust that goes beyond personalities. Transcending our separateness through the agency of relationship, is particularly important in Soto Zen.

> The disciple seeing Dechang is Dechang. Dechang guiding his disciple is meeting a true person.

When Dogen talks about dharma transmission he basically says that somebody could be enlightened and wise and mystical, but if they have not met and merged with another human being face-to face, there is an unrealized dimension to their lives. For

Dogen, that dimension is the most important dimension. There is something in us that cannot be awakened except through the agency of human relationship.

Suggested Practice: Catching

Reflect on whether you have one or more human relationships where you can communicate about things that are beyond words. About the really important matters: life, death, and awakening to reality.

· · · · · · · ·

> Beyond the limit of words, beyond the limit of the dualistic thinking that separates me from you, and from everything. Words do but point the way. But sometimes, a turning word in a true meeting with a wise teacher can change a life – as it once did mine. One phrase, free from distinction between "inhere" and "outthere," can become mutual awakening and catapult us into a Buddha-field that is beyond awakening.

· · · · · · · ·

> Beyond words, the eyes talk. I have several female friends, my brother and a former lover with whom I can communicate in silence, in the place beyond words, but this isn't an always thing; it's situational. The situation is out of the ordinary, someone is in pain or transition, great joy, great tragedy, a birth, a passing. In those moments, with those friends, nothing needs be said, we are connected in another way, on another plane of existence.

Week 51

Awakening Is Already in Us

It is not only that there is water in the world, but there is a world in water.

So we could say it is not only that your home is in the world, but the whole world is in your home. It is not just that you are in the whole world; the whole world is in you.

> There is a world of sentient beings in clouds. There is a world of sentient beings in the air. There is a world of sentient beings in fire. There is a world of sentient beings on earth. There is a world of sentient beings in the world of phenomena. There is a world of sentient beings in a blade of grass. There is a world of sentient beings in one staff. Wherever there is a world of sentient beings, there is a world of buddha-ancestors. Thoroughly examine the meaning of this.

Sentient beings are buddhas, the phenomenal world is the buddha realm, so in a way, we could forget about Buddha or Buddhism. It's not about that. It's about this human life, and its place in this world, and what life really and truly means, and how we really and truly live it. Awakening is programmed in the DNA. You don't have to manufacture it, or find it outside yourself. You just need to turn the light of awareness inwards.

I marvel at zazen. What a genius thing it is. When our whole lives are crashing, on our own, it would never occur to us to just sit down and breathe. But some people figured this out 2600 years ago in India. The Buddha spent 45 years creating support structures for this very simple act. Because of his effort, it has passed through cultures, been articulated in various ways, until now – we have it here.

> In this way, water is the true dragon's palace. It is not flowing downward. To regard water as only flowing is to slander water with the word 'flowing.' This would be the same as insisting that water does not flow.

Water doesn't only or always flow. Sometimes it's solid or a gaseous free-flow. It responds to conditions of temperature and gravity, taking the shape of its container.

> Water is just the true thusness of water. Water is water's complete characteristics; it is not flowing. When you investigate the flowing and not-flowing of a handful of water, thorough experience of all things is immediately actualized.
>
> There are mountains hidden in treasures. There are mountains hidden in swamps. There are mountains hidden in the sky. There are mountains hidden in mountains. There are mountains hidden in hiddenness. This is how we study.

Suggested Practice: Awakening Is Already In Us

Reflect on what this year has been for you. What mountains have you found hidden in your hiddenness?

• • • • • • • • •

Mountains are hidden in language. No looks like a big mountain, a barrier, protection from taking a chance. It is hard to find a clear path; the trail seems to keep going up but the path always ends in the same place. Yes is another mountain but to find it, I have to walk around No – through the brambles of fear of change and the challenge of finding something new. Once I found Yes, I started to climb – the path was clear and the view amazing.

This is the year I found Yes – it has been an exciting adventure and it has changed my self-image. Yes has also allowed me to close doors on things I was holding onto by opening a new vision. Every stage of my life has presented new challenges, opportunities but sometimes I would just play it safe. Now, in the last quadrant of my life, I want to explore and to do Yes. I have made the choice to climb Yes. I have no idea what is waiting ahead but I am walking up, looking for it, not wandering the trails of the lower mountain.

• • • • • • • •

I have loved the Rocky Mountains here in BC, and in Oregon, since I moved west to attend UBC in the late sixties, and I have always touched down into big mind when camping, hiking, backpacking or even just driving through them. Through this work of the last year my experience of the place where I live, my buddha realm, has deepened immeasurably, my valley has become my monastery, and because of our diligence in this project, I might be a little more of a bodhisattva than I was when we started.

Week 52

We Are Wildness

IT IS A VERY CRAZY, passionate thing, this human world we live in. The natural world is so sane. Gary Snyder, in *The Practice of the Wild*, says that wildness is another order of order. It is wild because we don't understand its order; it is so radically simple and so radically complex that we can't understand it, we can't figure it out.

It must be very exciting to be a scientist now – trying to figure out the nature of it all, joyfully studying, while knowing that you'll never figure it all out. You'll know more and more, but you will never come to the end of study. We can't understand wildness – that is what makes it wild. In other words, it has its own organizing systems. Even though on the one hand we say we are wrecking the planet, (and it's true, lowlands are flooding, forests are burning, droughts are spreading), the planet is doing fine. The planet knows how to handle what we do. She will swallow us up whole and then go on. The planet doesn't worry; we worry.

Dogen says that wildness is in us humans too. Not in the mind we have constructed or in the worlds we have constructed, but it is in us; it is not foreign to us, we are not separate from it. Practice is the effort to embrace our wildness and say, 'I don't understand. I will never understand or control it, but I can embrace it, I can l live it, I can know it is there, I can open my arms to it.'

And then we can be in accord with everything, like the rock that has been there for 20 million years. Things happen; the rock just bears it. It is the same thing with us. If we embrace our wildness, we can bear whatever happens, even our own death. And it is all ok.

But how do we not worry about the human world? I'm very worried. I'm worried about my friends, I'm worried about relatives and family, I'm worried about myself, I'm worried about our country, I'm worried about other countries. Where are human beings going? As many problems that it seems like we have, I have the feeling we are coming to a human crisis. We can't continue indulging this foolishness.

Let's say there are two kinds of worry – the kind of worry that makes us anxious and upset, and the kind of worry that we want to have – compassion, the activity of wisdom. Compassion is not being unconcerned. Compassion is exactly being concerned. If someone dies, I want to cry, even though I realize that it's just the way things are. Something comes; something goes. This goes on all the time, so it really is ok. The loss of a person in our lives is ok, on the one hand; on the other hand, I'm human. I naturally feel sorrow, I want to cry. I need to cry. Both sides are expressed in the teachings.

There is a false image of the sage who wanders forth, blithely happily, thinking, "Alive or dead, who knows?" But that image does not express the life that we live. That is not what practice proposes. Practice proposes that knowing that all is well is not incompatible with worrying about our peers.

Suggested Practice:
We Are Wildness

Do a closing ritual for this year long practice. Light a candle, do three full bows, blow out the candle and say aloud, "rest." Take a day off and then do zazen eternally.

Afterword

IF YOU HAVE READ THIS BOOK from beginning to end and wholeheartedly tried out even a few of the suggested practices it is likely that something has shifted in you. Norman's dharma talks are filled with 'turning words' – words that turn the mind that turns the world that turns the mind. You may have noticed a shift in the style and clarity of your awareness, you may have dropped into a mountain-like stability and be flowing more gently into a world that is becoming increasingly dangerous in these turbulent times.

Norman has brought a very poetic and often obscure text, one that contains many references to 8th century China and 13th century Japan, into a language that is accessible to we who are sustaining a zen practice in the west in the 21st Century. May we live its teachings and build civility into our families and communities in every interaction.

Before committing to publishing, I travelled through four mountain passes to ask Norman permission to publish this text. I carried with me a gigantic imposter syndrome; I felt like I had stolen his words. I carried a guilt and shame into dokusan that was deeply rooted in old familial karmic patterns. That was when Norman told me that his words didn't belong to him, they belonged to his teachers.

I was very emotional when I entered dokusan, very expressive of those difficult and, for me, noisy, high energy emotions. Towards the end of our meeting, when I had calmed down, I asked Norman if doing dokusan morning noon and night, as he had been doing for six continuous days in the 2018 Mountain Rain Zen Community's Annual Loon Lake sesshin, was exhausting. He said, "No. I just see flashes of lightening coming and going." In that moment, I could see that he is mountain, constant, aware and emanating the suchness of mountains and rivers.

I'm excited to send these teachings into the world, and am humbled by the opportunity and my ability to do so. My thanks to John Negru, publisher at Sumeru Books, for sitting like a mountain as he helped me though my first book publishing experience.

www.ingramcontent.com/pod-product-compliance
Lightning Source LLC
Chambersburg PA
CBHW030142170426
43199CB00008B/170